HEALING

from a TOXIC
and ABUSIVE
RELATIONSHIP

A Journey of Self-Reflection and Recovery

GREYSON JAMES

outskirts
press

Maybe you went through
it and survived just so
you could help someone
else make it through.

Table of Contents

Introduction

Being on the receiving end of mental and emotional abuse is a life-altering and emotionally devastating experience that no one should have to go through. It's not something you were looking for when you allowed your heart to be opened as you entered the relationship with your abuser, filled with the hope that this person could be the answer to all of your dreams. You had no reason to believe otherwise. After all, it's not like your abuser was wearing a sign around their neck advertising the fact that he/she was going to abuse you and change your life forever – in a bad way.

You had no reason to believe that they would try to hurt, control and manipulate you until you no longer knew who you were anymore. You probably had no idea that there were predators (both male and female) who were devoid of the ability to feel emotions the way most normal people do. That they could fastidiously present themselves in a way that would not only encourage you to let your guard down and allow them to infiltrate your life, but also take advantage of you and tear your life apart. A predator with the incredible ability to mimic all of your desires and emotions in such a convincing way, that you couldn't possibly imagine them being the devious and soulless abuser that they really are.

When most people think of or hear about abuse, it's usually physical. That's because it is fairly easy to identify and can be outwardly seen. But the pain one can feel from mental and emotional abuse runs deep and can often cause as much, if not more trauma than physical wounds can. I'm not minimizing the wounds inflicted from physical abuse, because it is horrible and often leaves scars. It's just that most physical wounds will eventually heal, while emotional trauma can stay with you for quite some time and leaves its own invisible scars. It can have an impact on who you are as a person, and it can affect the way you think and your ability to process emotions and heal. The more abuse you are exposed to, the greater impact it can have on you, and the longer it can take to recover from those wounds and become healthy again.

I personally experienced almost four years of severe emotional and mental abuse, not to mention the manipulation that came with it. My exposure to this abuse almost killed me. My abuser was a hall of famer that embodied all four of the Cluster B personality disorders including antisocial, borderline, histrionic, and narcissistic personality disorders. And it took me still more than three years before I was able to break away from her.

In my first book - *Surviving A Toxic and Abusive Relationship*, I shared how a person can get sucked into an abusive relationship – how you are first idealized, then devalued, then severely abused until finally, one day you start to understand what has happened to you and you slowly gain the courage to escape. I also shared how emotional abusers will try to isolate you from everyone you know and care about and how over time their abuse can cause you to lose all sense of personal identity and self-esteem.

I have traveled the road from victim to survivor, and by the grace of God my wounds have finally healed. It's been a long but incredible faith-filled journey, with many hard and painful decisions, conflicting emotions, and lots of learning about abuse, my abuser and also myself.

I'm still alive to talk about it, share what I've learned, and hopefully help and guide others, (male or female), to do the same. Like me, I'm pretty sure it wasn't your intention to end up in an emotionally abusive relationship, but there are ways to heal and help you bounce back. This can enable you to discover and embrace all that God desires for you going forward.

Abuse. That word alone conjures up all sorts of different and unpleasant images. Most people probably think they have a basic idea or understanding of the definition of abuse, but let's take a little deeper look at what it actually can be. According to Merriam Webster's Dictionary, abuse can be defined as

1. use (something) to bad effect or for a bad purpose *misuse*. Similar: misapply, mishandle, exploit, pervert, *take advantage of*
2. treat something or someone with cruelty or violence, especially *regularly* or **repeatedly.** Similar: mistreat, *treat badly*, misuse, handle/treat roughly, interfere with, assault, hit, injure, hurt, harm, damage, wrong, bully, persecute, oppress
3. the improper use of something, *improper* or *excessive* use or treatment.
4. *language that condemns* or vilifies usually unjustly, intemperately, and angrily.
5. physical maltreatment, *to use* or treat so as *to injure or damage*.
6. a deceitful act: *deception*

As one can see, the definition for the act of abuse is not that simple. It can also be experienced in a number of different forms including physical, verbal, sexual, mental/psychological, financial, legal, or spiritual, but in all cases it is *intentional* and definitely leads to, and includes emotional abuse.

But emotionally abusive *behavior* expands those things to a much different level, and includes accusing, blaming, humiliation, negating, criticizing, controlling, emotional neglect, isolation, shaming and denial. You can also throw in intentional infliction of emotional pain or intimidation through verbal or non-verbal acts along with a denial of a person's civil rights just to be more inclusive and thorough.

While we now have a pretty good definition of the various forms of abuse, we still need to look at what abuse actually means to those involved, which is *control*. When a truly abusive situation exists, it's because one party (the abuser) is seeking to control the other (the victim) through abuse. Abuse is derived from force, manipulation and repetition and exists when one person has more power and control than the other. Abuse doesn't allow for changed behavior; it forces it. And no person has the right to exercise control over someone else or force another person's behavior.

Abuse has become an enormous problem in the United States. Nearly one-in-three adult women and nearly one-in-four adult men have reported experiencing physical, sexual or mental abuse or Intimate Partner Violence (IPV) in their lifetime. For emotional abuse, the prevalence rates are even higher, with 40% of women and 32% of men reporting expressive aggression, verbal abuse or emotional violence and more than 40% of both men and women reporting they have experienced some form of coercive control from their partners.

They Call It Abuse for a Reason

The fact is that many mental and emotional abusers are really, really good at what they do. Most of their victims don't have a clue that they are truly being abused until they have been damaged in ways that they often have difficulty recovering from. This is because in addition to the physical symptoms such as headaches, stomach aches, eating and sleeping disorders that develop over time, most victims are often left with a nasty case of Post-Traumatic Stress Disorder (PTSD), anxiety disorder, depression, shame and emotional distress. You don't just get over those overnight. And the longer you are exposed to the toxic behavior and abuse, the longer it takes to heal from it.

Most victims take a while just to realize and admit that they are being abused. Then you often experience rationalization and denial in its many wonderful forms as you contemplate leaving your abuser. It can take months or even years from this point in the abuse cycle before you experience that one final, painful and heartbreaking event that tips the scales and makes you finally take that definitive step to leave.

You will most likely wrestle with the guilt, shame and regret that comes with not only being on the receiving end of abuse but also making the decision to leave the relationship. And what follows is a long, emotion-filled period of contemplation and soul-searching, looking for answers to hundreds of questions of how you got into the relationship in the first place and then allowed yourself to be abused in so many horrible ways, and for so long.

The questions can range from ones of personal reflection to focusing on your abuser and why they treated you the way they did. Questions such as:

- Why did it take me so long to recognize the abuse?
- Why was I in denial about the abuse for so long?
- Why did I stay in the relationship so long?
- Why did I allow or put up with the abuse?
- What is wrong with me?
- What did I do to provoke the abuse?
- Why did my abuser do this to me?
- Why did my abuser deny their abuse?
- Am I to blame for the abuse I received?
- Why do I still love my abuser?

- Where is/was God through all of this?
- Who am I and what do I do now?
- Will I ever heal?
- Will these feelings ever go away?
- Is there any hope for my future?

Once you get through this very important period of reflection, you can actually start on a path toward healing. And I promise there will be many wonderful discoveries along the way. You will learn that the abuse was *not* your fault. You will discover you are not alone and that many people have suffered and experienced some of the same pains and emotions you have.

You will discover the brokenness in your abuser that caused them to treat you (and probably others before you) so horribly the way they did. You will learn that there is no excuse for their toxic, abusive and dysfunctional behavior, but you will gain a better understanding of it. This can help you develop an empathy toward them that will hopefully allow you to eventually forgive the incredible pain they caused you.

You will discover that there is a Father in Heaven whose heart broke for you while you were suffering; uniquely wired you to withstand and survive the abuse; and is so proud of who you are and how you are going to come out of the situation from which you escaped. Most importantly, I want to help you grow more confident and discover just how strong and resilient you actually are. You will recover from this painful period in your life and you will be able to learn from your discoveries. You will go from being a victim to an informed survivor. And you will be able to hold your head high and move forward again.

Identifying Abuse

There comes a point in every abusive relationship when the person being abused starts to come to terms with the dysfunctional and toxic behavior of their abuser. Sometimes it's things that you previously dismissed as aberrations that suddenly capture your attention. Sometimes it's the doubts that have been lingering in the back of your mind for some time, that start to come to the forefront and you are hit with the reality that what you are experiencing is not normal, let alone healthy. It can often be a sudden undeniable fact that you discover and cannot argue with, dismiss or excuse.

It could be a comment from a friend or family member that you've been pondering that finally hits home. It could be the ceaseless repetition and regularity of the toxic behavior that finally takes its toll. It could be an item of yours that has been taken, broken or gone missing. It could be the isolation you constantly feel that you no longer can take or accept anymore. It could be money that has been stolen from you. It could be the latest insult hurled at you, a friend or a family member that you just won't tolerate anymore. It could be a particularly painful incident that finally makes you reach your breaking point.

Sometimes it's just that you get tired of hurting, you get tired of being tired or more accurately, you get tired of being exhausted. Tired of making excuses about your abuser to your family or friends, and that's if you still have any that your abuser hasn't removed from your life. Tired of the headaches, lack of sleep and that constant knot in your stomach. Tired of walking on pins and needles around your abuser wondering what will trigger their next explosion, when it comes. And it always does, like clock-work. You can count on it. You might be tired of the insults, manipulation, jealousy, lies and gaslighting. Tired of trying to defend yourself. Tired of it all.

But how do you get to that point and why does it take so long to get there? How and when do you know unequivocally that what you are experiencing and have been tolerating is abuse? Emotional abuse can be so emotionally draining and confusing, and can look so different from one person to the next. Physical abuse is instantly recognizable, you feel it, it hurts and hopefully doesn't leave a fleshly scar. It's terrible, should never be tolerated or minimized, and is truly horrific in nature. But emotional and mental abuse takes longer to sink in and recognize, and the damage it can do to a person on the receiving end of it can linger for years.

And to make things even more confusing is the fact that mental and emotional abuse each have their own unique qualities that do their damage. They are often used interchangeably because of their similar characteristics and effects on their victims. But despite some of the similarities, there are unique differences between the two.

Mental abuse involves the use of verbal and social tactics in order to control someone's way of *thinking*. A mental abuser will often convince the victim that they are crazy, manipulate them, or make harmful threats against them. Emotional abuse involves controlling someone's way of *feeling*. Both can cause intense and long-lasting mental trauma. An emotional abuser will often demean their victim, engage in victim blaming, and cause their victim to undergo intense humiliation while a mental abuser has a greater effect on a victim's mental capacity, causing them to question themselves and make them feel like they are incapable or even gradually losing their mind.

And when you have an emotional abuser that is skilled at combining the two, you have a lethal cocktail of abuse that can leave you questioning your very existence and purpose in life. Because many abusers incorporate both mental and emotional abuse in their arsenal, both behaviors fall under the heading of emotional abuse.

Regardless of whether they engage in one or both types of abuse, an emotional abuser's goal is to undermine the other person's feelings of self-worth and independence. It can be as destructive and damaging to a victim as physical abuse, and its primary goal is to gain and maintain power and control over someone. And just to add a little spice to the mix, emotional abuse is often accompanied by other types of abuse including financial, sexual, spiritual and physical abuse.

What Is Emotional Abuse?

Emotional abuse includes any attempt by one person in a marriage or intimate relationship to dominate and control the other. The aim of emotional abuse is to chip away at your feelings of self-worth and independence. It uses fear, guilt, shame, and intimidation to wear you down, often leaving you feeling defeated and hopeless as if there's no way out of the relationship, or that without your abusive partner, you will be left with nothing.

Emotional abuse is often minimized or overlooked - even by the person on the receiving end who is experiencing it. Both men and women can suffer from emotional abuse, and it can involve any of the following:

- **Verbal Abuse**: Overreacting, arguing, yelling at you, insulting you or swearing at you.
- **Rejection**: Constantly dismissing or rejecting your thoughts, ideas, opinions, accomplishments.
- **Gaslighting**: Making you doubt your own feelings and thoughts, and even your sanity, by manipulating the truth.
- **Put-downs**: Calling you names, attacking your intelligence,

looks or capabilities. Publicly embarrassing you or humiliating you. This is also called social abuse.

- **The Silent Treatment**: Ignoring you, glaring at you and refusing to talk to you.
- **Threats**: Yelling or sulking, threatening you or making you feel intimidated.
- **Isolation**: Limiting your freedom of movement, stopping you from contacting other people (such as friends or family). It can also prevent you from doing the things you normally enjoy doing.
- **Financial Abuse**: Controlling or withholding your money, preventing you from working or studying, stealing from you, or excessively spending your money.
- **Intimidation**: Purposely and repeatedly saying or doing things that are intended to hurt you.
- **Possessiveness**: Controlling where you go and who you see, what you're doing and who you're doing it with.
- **Jealousy**: Accuse you of flirting or being unfaithful, behaving rudely in front of friends or family.
- **Comparisons**: Constantly compare you unfavorably to former lovers and others.
- **Blame Shifting**: Blaming you for all the problems in the relationship, their own abusive behavior and everything else they can think of.
- **Monitoring**: Your calls, messages and emails. Tracking your phone or car. Demanding passwords to your phone, email or social media.
- **Pathological Lying**: Making confusing and contradictory statements, long, convoluted and excessive explanations. Nothing they say adds up or makes any sense at all.

Other Signs of an Abusive Relationship

In addition to the major signs of emotional abuse, there is the effect that it has on your feelings and emotions. That's why they call it *emotional* abuse. How does the behavior of your abuser make you feel?

- Do you feel like you have to walk on eggshells or trying to dodge pins and needles around them?
- Are you constantly watching what you say and do in order to avoid a blow-up?
- Do you feel that you can't do anything right for your abuser?
- Are you afraid of your abuser or their reactions much of the time?
- Do you avoid certain topics out of fear of angering your abuser?
- Have you started to believe that you deserve to be hurt or mistreated?
- Do you wonder if you are imagining things or going crazy?
- Do you feel emotionally numb and helpless?

The Impact of Emotional Abuse

If you answered yes to even one of these questions, chances are you are in an unhealthy and emotionally abusive relationship. You may think that physical abuse is far worse than emotional abuse, since physical violence can send you to the hospital and leave you with physical wounds. But the consequences of emotional abuse can be just as damaging—sometimes even more so. That's because the scars of emotional abuse are real. They run deep and are long-lasting. This negative impact on your self-esteem and confidence can lead to anxiety, and leave you feeling depressed, anxious, helpless, alone or even suicidal.

Emotional abuse can happen to anyone--men or women, it does not discriminate. It occurs within all age ranges, ethnic backgrounds, and economic levels. No one should ever have to feel like they should accept it. Everyone deserves to feel loved, valued, respected and safe. No one should have to endure the kind of pain that comes from abuse of any kind, and your first step to breaking free is recognizing that your relationship is unhealthy and that your spouse or partner is abusive.

2

Overcoming Denial

Perhaps the greatest impediment to leaving a mentally or emotionally abusive relationship is our denial that it is actually happening to us. That's because denial is a defense mechanism that helps us cope with things that are unpleasant or are hurting us. There are many reasons why we might subconsciously use denial, including avoidance of physical or emotional pain, fear, shame, conflict or consequences. In fact, we're actually wired to deny for our survival. Think about a child who denies having colored the wall of their room with crayons but has the colors of crayons smeared all over their hands. That child is denying they did it out of self-preservation and the fear of being punished.

As adults, denial can often help us adapt or cope with difficult, unpleasant or painful emotions. It allows our body and mind to adjust to the grief, shock or pain we are experiencing more gradually. Where it becomes unhealthy, is when we employ it out of fear or to avoid having to deal with something we know is not good for us or to avoid the consequences of our own or someone else's actions or behavior. It's not adaptive when we deny the warning signs of a treatable illness, abusive and disrespectful behavior, or a problem out of fear.

Familiarity

Sometimes we deny abuse that is obvious because it feels familiar. We know the toxic and dysfunctional behavior is hurtful, disrespectful and doesn't make us feel good, but we put up with it anyway because we have become used to it, rationalize that it couldn't possibly be better with someone else or away from it, or we fear what might happen to us if we leave our abuser.

As strange as that may sound, this response is actually quite common amongst victims of abusers. It's just not healthy. And if we don't deny the actual action and how it makes us feel, we often will minimize the behavior as not being as bad as it really is, along with minimizing how bad it makes us feel and the effect or toll it is taking on our health and emotions.

Inner Conflict

This often happens because of the conflict of emotions that we feel inside of ourselves. You may truly love your abuser like I did, and you might even have become addicted to the love they first showed you earlier in the relationship. You may have become dependent on them because they are the main or only breadwinner in the relationship and you feel powerless to leave them. Sometimes it's easier to forget, rationalize, or make excuses for your abuser and their toxic behavior than accept the unthinkable reality that you are actually being abused.

Sometimes it's easier to blame ourselves than face the reality of our situation. We often deny the truth of something when it might mean we have to take an action we don't want to take. We search for other explanations to explain away the behavior we don't want to have to deal with. We don't want to confront the truth that is staring us in the face because it would force us to not only face the pain of the betrayal, humiliation and disrespect we already feel, but also the loss from leaving the relationship or getting a divorce.

Shame

One of the things we may not realize when we are in a state of denial, is that it often comes from a place of feeling shame about the relationship we are in. Shame is an extremely painful emotion and can really affect our way of thinking. Many people who have been involved in abusive relationships, (including myself) don't realize how much shame can drive our lives even if our self-esteem is normally pretty good. That's because abuse can severely alter the way we feel about ourselves. We don't want anyone to see how much we are hurting or we are embarrassed that we got ourselves into an abusive relationship that feels out of our control. Abuse can do immense damage to one's confidence and it can make a person feel worthless.

Fear

Another primary reason people remain in denial is fear. Perhaps you're afraid that if you confront the problems in your relationship, you may start down a path that ultimately leads to the end of your marriage or relationship. You may be concerned that your abuser will become enraged if you suddenly stand up for yourself. You may be afraid you will discover more secrets or truths about your abuser and the reasons behind their behavior.

If you have children, you might be concerned about exposing them to the abuse. You may be afraid you'll discover that your spouse or partner has been or is being unfaithful. You may be afraid you will discover that your abuser is stealing from you. Any of these fears can compel a person to avoid facing some scary issues in life.

Denying Your Needs

Feeling ashamed about ourselves often leads us to deny our own needs or rationalize that we don't deserve the things we truly need. One can get to the point in which you just accept the way things are and you convince yourself that you actually are getting your needs met. You just don't understand why you constantly live with such an empty feeling inside of yourself. This is because your relationship has probably become primarily if not completely focused on meeting your abusive partner/spouse's needs, and rarely if ever on meeting any of your own.

The sad fact is that your needs are probably rarely considered anymore if at all. In fact, you will probably doubt that your abuser even thinks you have any needs because all they will ever be focused on is their own. Personal insecurity is at the heart of every abuser's behavior, and they will always place their own highly demanding emotional, physical, financial and materialistic needs over yours in every circumstance.

You will eventually realize that your relationship is all about them and not about you. There is no "us" in your relationship, just a "them." Sadly, you may have reached the point where you have trained yourself to ignore your needs and desires and draw satisfaction from the few times that you do something right that actually pleases them.

Denial of needs is often a major reason emotional abuse victims remain unhappy in relationships. We train ourselves to deny our problems, needs and feelings that are not being met. This is often done subconsciously to the point that we are not even aware of it. You just suddenly realize one day that you have an immense feeling of emptiness and unfulfillment.

You may also feel a guilt or lack the courage or capability to ask for what you need or express how you need to get your needs met. You will discover later on that learning to identify and express your feelings and needs is a major part of recovery and is essential to your personal well-being and enjoyment of a truly satisfying relationship.

Types and Degrees of Denial

Being in denial doesn't always mean we can't or don't see that there is a problem. It's just a human response that helps us excuse, minimize or rationalize its significance or effect upon us. On a deeper level, we may repress things that are too painful to remember or think about. But denial harms us when it causes us to ignore problems for which there are solutions, or to deny feelings and needs that if dealt with, would enhance our lives. And we often use denial in varying degrees.

- **First degree:** We deny that the problem, symptom, feeling or need exists.
- **Second degree:** We minimize or rationalize the problem or behavior.
- **Third degree:** We admit there is a problem, but we deny the consequences of it.
- **Fourth degree:** We are unwilling to ask for help to deal with or respond to it.

Denial can take many forms, but the two main types of denial are suppression and repression. With suppression, the person who is being abused has some memory or acknowledgment of the abuse, but they seek to ignore the meaning of the information they are processing. Although all of the thoughts and information about the abuse are available to them, the victim will try to block them out to keep them from entering from the subconscious to the conscious part of their brain.

If the abuse does become clearer, the person will become skilled at controlling or suppressing the thoughts surrounding the instances of abuse. When denial is in the form of repression, the victim of the abuse has no conscious recall of the event(s) or behavior. It stays in the unconscious part of the victim's brain and has an effect on them. They just don't have the ability to realize it or the damage it is doing to them.

How to Know If You're in Denial

Sometimes it's not easy to recognize if denial is holding you back. The types of denial you experience can change depending on the moment or type of abuse you are experiencing. There are a number of ways to recognize if you are in denial about the state of your relationship and the abuse you are receiving from your partner or spouse. I actually consider them signs that you can't and shouldn't ignore. Do you:

- Often think about how you wish things could/should be in your relationship?
- Wonder, "If only my partner/spouse would . . ."?
- Cast doubt on or dismiss your own feelings? Does your abuser?
- Hide embarrassing aspects of your relationship from your friends and family?
- Dread talking about problems or how you feel about the way you are treated?
- Continue to believe repeated broken assurances or promises from your abuser?
- Hope that some special event will somehow improve your relationship?
- Constantly make concessions to your abuser or try to placate them?
- Feel resentful toward or feel used by your partner/spouse?
- Keep waiting/hoping for your relationship to improve or your abuser to change?

Moving Past Denial

If you answered yes to any of these questions, you are probably in some state of denial. You might finally be at that point where you are coming to grips with the idea that something is seriously wrong in your relationship. You might finally be realizing that you are in an intolerable situation with a toxic and abusive person. And the most important and self-loving thing you can do for yourself right now is to commit to honestly explore and understand why you are feeling so confused, troubled and sad.

You might need time to work through the memories and realizations of what has happened to you and make the changes needed to get out from under the emotional abuse you have been experiencing. No matter what, it's important to realize that remaining in denial won't change the reality of your situation.

You may have reached this point of realization but still feel stuck regarding what to do about it. I want to encourage you to honestly examine what it is that you fear. Give yourself the freedom to express your fears and emotions. Consider writing them down on paper so you can see them and grapple with them. Are there irrational feelings or beliefs that you have about facing your situation? What are the potential negative consequences of not taking any action to address your abuser's behavior or to not get out of your relationship? Write down all of your thoughts and truly examine them.

If you can't make progress dealing with this stressful situation on your own, I want to encourage you to reach out to a trusted friend or family member and share your feelings about these questions with them. A professional therapist can also be of great assistance in helping you overcome your denial and help in your recovery by pointing out your defenses, questioning contradictions between your thoughts and reality, helping you identify your denied feelings and needs, and supporting you in facing your fears and inner conflicts and in making changes. They can also help you find healthy ways to cope with and move forward from your situation rather than trying to pretend it doesn't exist.

Usually, the longer you have suppressed or denied the abuse, the longer it will take for the denial phase to end. And staying in the denial stage can be costly. It stifles your creativity and prevents you from thinking spontaneously because you are placing all of your energy into censoring your feelings and avoiding remembering and dealing with the memories of the abuse.

Keeping things suppressed requires a lot of energy that could be freed for helping yourself recover and heal from the abuse. It may take a lot of hard work, but if you are working with a counselor in a safe environment, you will eventually be able to allow these memories to emerge, understand why and how they happened, and come to grips with how your abuser's toxic behavior has negatively affected your life.

3

Why Abusers Abuse

One of the reasons an abuse victim often has trouble coming to terms with their denial, is that they often either blame themselves for their abuser's behavior, or falsely believe that their abuser can't help or control their own behavior. We tend to give our partner or spouse the benefit of the doubt when they harm us and act like the only reason they lashed out was because it was a *reaction* to something we said or did wrong, or that they just couldn't control their response that was triggered by something outside of their control. In doing so, the victim often overlooks the fact that most human beings would never act or respond that way.

Abusive Behavior Is a Choice

Despite what many people and especially many victims believe, domestic violence and emotional abuse does not take place because an abuser "loses control" over their behavior or is simply "reacting." That's because abusive behavior is a deliberate choice by the abuser to gain control over their victims. And they will use a variety of tactics to manipulate you and exert their power over you. For the abuser, it has been and always will be, about their ability to have control over you, not their lack of it over themselves.

They are *fully* aware of everything they are doing and the pain it is causing you. That's because their goal is to have full and complete dominance over every single part of your life and your marriage or relationship with them. Abusers are experienced at the art of manipulation and control, and they always have an end goal in mind. The rest of us don't think the way they do. We can't even fathom the type of behavior we encounter until we are taken by surprise and encounter it. And they have a number of different ways they use to gain the control over you they so desperately desire.

- **Dominance**. Abusive individuals have an insatiable need to feel in charge of the relationship. They may make decisions for you, tell you what to do or what's best for you, and expect you to obey without question. Your abuser may treat you like a servant, child, or even as their personal possession. Regardless of how they treat you, they will try and make you feel inferior to them in every way possible. Their goal is to make you believe that you couldn't possibly live your life without them.
- **Humiliation**. Your abuser will do everything they can to lower your self-esteem or make you feel defective in some way. They have no problem hurling insults at you, calling you names, shaming and guilting you and putting you down in front of others, especially friends and family. They will not hesitate to pull out every weapon in their toxic arsenal to erode your self-worth and make you feel powerless. And once they've convinced you that you are worthless, and no one else would want you, you're less likely to leave.
- **Isolation**. Your abusive partner will do everything they can to cut you off from your family, friends and the outside world. They will question everything you do, everyone you speak with, and anywhere you go. They will monitor your calls, texts and emails and even track your whereabouts. And all of this is designed to make you more dependent on them.
- **Threats**. Emotional abusers will commonly use threats to

keep their partners from leaving. Your abuser may threaten to hurt you physically or financially, spread untrue rumors about you, your children, friends or family members, file fake charges against you, or threaten to commit suicide. And they won't hesitate or allow a week to go by in which they don't let you know that they are constantly thinking about leaving you or considering divorcing you.

- **Silent Treatment.** There is a tortuous aspect to silent treatment. It is used to make you feel stupid, inadequate and rejected when you are shunned for a long period of time. Abusers often do this to boost their own ego because the shunned partner is now focusing all of their attention on the abuser, trying to either figure out what they might have done wrong, or what they need to do to stop the behavior. The other thing it does, is that it sends a clear message to the person being abused that they are bad, stupid or crazy and definitely not worthy of their abuser's attention.

Abusers *are* able to control their behavior - they do it all the time. Yes, in the cases of some people who suffer from Borderline Personality Disorder (BPD), some of their outbursts are part of their overreaction to something, but they are always fully aware of their reactions at the time they make them, and yet they rarely take responsibility for them after, let alone apologize for their behavior.

The fact is, emotional abusers pick and choose whom they want to abuse and when they want to do it, especially the narcissistic ones. They don't just randomly insult, threaten, or assault everyone in their life who gives them grief. They do it to the individuals they have selected who have or represent something they desire and who they believe they can control and dominate. They also do it to the people who are closest to them, the ones they claim to love.

Unless they are trying to publicly insult or humiliate you in front of others, they will normally save most of their abuse for when you are alone and no one else is around to witness their behavior. Think about that for a minute. It takes a tremendous amount of control and planning to decide when they are going to abuse you. And they are only going to stop their toxic behavior when it benefits them to do so, like when the police show up, their boss calls or a friend or family member stops by to visit.

The Cycles of Emotional Abuse

By now you have probably come to realize that while you may experience emotional abuse on a daily basis, most of it will fall into a distinct and common pattern or cycle of behavior. Within each cycle, you will experience a period (often around a week) of outbursts, extreme nastiness, and blaming followed by shunning and silent treatment and then finally a period of relative quiet until the cycle repeats itself.

Within each abuse cycle will be the actual incidents that continuously make up the cycle, and they in turn have a distinct cycle too. First, your abuser will lash out at you in whatever shape or form they have chosen for that particular moment to make the greatest impact. Then they will rationalize their behavior to you, make excuses and then assign blame (normally on you).

Once they are satisfied with the amount of pain they have inflicted on you, they may act as if nothing has happened. They may actually choose to show you some modicum of affection, act seductive or turn on just enough charm to give you hope that they have really changed this time. Your abuser's loving gestures in between the episodes of abuse are designed to make you think twice about leaving them. They may cause you to believe that you are the only person who can help them, that they will change their behavior, and that they truly love you.

However, the dangers of staying in the relationship are very real. In reality your abuser has probably already begun to think about new ways to abuse, hurt and manipulate you. Because they are so unhappy within themselves, they will spend a lot of time looking for things they believe you are doing wrong and how they will make you pay for it. They will set you up, and then put their plan in motion to create the next situation where they can justify abusing you again.

And all of this can be even worse and more confusing if your abuser claims to be a Christian. That is because their supposed faith will make it even harder for you to reconcile their abusive behavior with their declared faith. And abuse goes so far against what God had in mind for relationships, especially marriage. Any husband/wife/partner who genuinely loves, understands and is intimate with the one true God, will not treat their spouse or partner in harsh or destructive ways.

Ephesians 5:25 makes it perfectly clear that "Husbands should love their wives, as Christ loved the church and gave himself up for her." And Ephesians 5:33 and Titus 2:4 clearly state that a wife should love and be respectful of her husband. Both men and women are given clear instructions. There's no room for ambiguity. And 1 Corinthians 7:3 goes further by stating that:

> "The husband must fulfill his duty to his wife, and likewise also the wife to her husband."

There's no way you can twist that to mean anything else. Otherwise, you have a heart problem.

Any husband, wife or partner who truly understands God's love will extend and apply the same love and grace that God shows us, to their own spouse or partner. Titus 2:2 specifically instructs men to "be temperate, dignified and sensible," and Titus 2:5 specifically instructs women to "be sensible, pure and kind." A Christian believer is supposed to have the mind of Christ. And this should be displayed outwardly through their actions. Because being a true follower of Jesus demands that you think more highly of others than you do yourself, placing the needs of others over your own. (Philippians 2:4)

Any Christian's true theology should be visible in how they treat, speak to, and sacrifice for their spouse/partner. A person who claims to love, know and follow Jesus will not mistreat, demoralize, or abuse those they claim to love, let alone anyone else. That's because abuse is a behavior that mars the image of Christ and His healthy design for covenant relationships. Anyone who claims to walk in the Spirit will not degrade, defraud, destroy or attack another person's soul. They are to be Holy (1 Peter 1:13-25 and 2:1-3). So anyone who abuses others is NOT a true follower of Jesus Christ. And don't let anyone tell you or try and convince you otherwise.

Why Abusers Deny Their Behavior

Abusers are notorious for not taking any responsibility for their actions and are very adept at making excuses for everything they do, including their atrocious and inexcusable, toxic behavior. When emotional abusers are confronted with allegations of abuse, they usually deny that the abuse ever happened, or they downplay the severity of their actions and responses. They won't hesitate to blame their behavior on you, their childhood, a bad day, your children, the pets, your friends or other family members. Their behavior will always be someone else's fault.

This can often make the people on the receiving end of the abuse feel angry, confused and hopeless. You may wonder why most abusers not only choose to deny their behavior, but they often do it with such an unshakable belief that they have done nothing wrong. There are a number of reasons for abusers to deny their behavior, and often the abuser relies on all of them at different times to excuse what they have done or to pretend it never happened.

For starters, emotional abusers (especially narcissists), are very adept at convincing the rest of the world around them that they have done nothing wrong. A common tactic that abusers use is playing the role of the victim. This way people will feel sympathy for them, and hold the victim accountable for the abuse that occurred, not the abuser. Some can even manipulate the victim into believing that they are responsible for the abuse and that they mistreated the abuser. While it can be hard to fight this manipulation, it is important to remember that they are always at fault for the abuse, not you.

Sadly, many abusers have grown up in abusive and dysfunctional family environments and were either taught or learned to believe that abusive behavior is acceptable. And this can affect both the abuser and the victim. And making things even more difficult is the fact that most abusive people have held this belief for a long time. But this certainly doesn't excuse the abuse.

Some abusers will claim that they do not remember the moments of abuse. A possible explanation for this is that they engage in these actions so often, they may not remember specific incidents. To them, abuse is just part of a normal routine and has happened many times. There are also theories that some abusers are able to block or alter their memory of an abusive event out of guilt or from a deep-seated subconscious belief that their behavior wasn't actually abusive or nearly as severe in nature as their victim claims it to be.

Emotional abusers will often also deny responsibility for their behavior by claiming it was simply an accident or was caused from stress, drinking too much or just having a bad day. This allows them to claim that their actions were only in response to something or someone else (you). They may also downplay their actions by saying that the victim was deserving of their abusive treatment because of something they did.

Some abusers will act like their victims are keeping score of their outbursts and abusive behavior and that an "incident" is simply a negative entry on the ledger. Because most abusers think so highly of themselves (on the outside), they will truly believe that they have so many good behavior entries on the ledger that they can justify indulging in the bad ones "every now and then." These are the same abusers who will often say things like, "*You're so lucky to have someone like me*" or "*It isn't nearly all bad*" to cover for abuse that needs to be confessed and addressed.

But for most emotional abusers, they simply play down the event or deny the abuse took place to avoid being held accountable for their actions. It's easy enough to understand that people sometimes lie to try to save themselves from having to endure the consequences of what they have created. And with abusers, lying isn't all that difficult because their perceptions and their sense of right and wrong are already warped in the first place.

Some abusers truly believe that they are good persons, even angelic and better than most, and therefore believe that they do not abuse people. Some abusers have convinced themselves that abuse only occurs if it is physical in nature or that there is a hierarchy of abuse and that theirs is on the lower end of severity. There is often a disconnect between their abusive behavior and what they actually believe they did. This conflict between their belief and actions allows them to deny or minimize the abuse and maintain their rigid belief that they are still good persons.

I'm not sharing this information to excuse or protect any abuser's behavior. I just found that understanding this aspect of emotional abuse helped with my own healing after being abused. Through all of the pain I went through, I never understood why my abuser would either blatantly deny her behavior and what she had done to me, pretended it never happened, downplayed her behavior or would blame me for it. Gaining a better understanding of this brought me comfort, and I hope it does for you as well. Victims of abuse are not crazy, and they don't just imagine the abuse they received. It was real, it happened, and it matters. And no amount of denial or minimizing will excuse their abuser's toxic behavior.

4

It's Not Your Fault

One of the truly sad aspects of being on the receiving end of abuse, is that survivors often go through periods of doubt and self-blame after they finally find the strength to leave an abusive relationship. Your mind will be filled with a ton of complex and often conflicting emotions. You may feel afraid, confused, ashamed, angry, guilty, relieved, sad, happy, or hopeful. You may blame yourself or feel responsible for some of what happened in your relationship. You may wonder what you could have done, or if you could have done more to fix it. You might feel bad that you couldn't fix it. You may wonder what is wrong with you, that you could stay in the relationship for so long or allowed your abuser to use and manipulate you.

Among the most common questions survivors often ask are things like:

- Was it my fault?
- Why couldn't I stop it?
- Why did I tolerate the abuse for so long?
- Why did I choose to ignore or overlook the toxic behavior for so long?
- Was I really so unlovable?
- Why didn't I know that it was wrong?

- Could I have done something differently to make them love me?
- Could I have done something differently to make them stop hurting me?
- Is there something about me that brought out the worst in them?
- Why did this happen to me?
- Why did I allow this to happen to me?
- Why did I cover up their abusive behavior to others?
- Why do I feel guilty for leaving my abuser?
- Should I have given the relationship more time?
- Should I have given my abuser more chances to get help and get better?
- Why didn't I leave sooner?
- Could I have loved them better?

The thoughts can go on and on.

Deep down inside your heart you know what they did was wrong. It was wrong of them to scream and yell at you constantly. It was wrong of them to ignore you. Wrong to isolate, control, confuse and manipulate you. Wrong to monitor your phone, emails and social media. Wrong to steal from you, withhold money from you, call you names, gaslight you, blame you for their actions, hurt or punish you. It was wrong of them to cheat on you, sneak around behind your back, talk bad about you, embarrass you, and question you . . . about everything.

Sometimes the victim-blaming comes from a still, small voice that speaks to you while you are thinking about things. Other times it might just be a random, gentle whisper in the back of your mind. And sometimes it might scream at you loud and clear, triggering an all-consuming shaming sequence that you can't get out of your tired and confused mind. Sometimes it can be a well-meaning suggestion from a friend that starts out with the words "*You should have*" that sends you back down the road of remembrance, regret and reflection.

If this is your reality, there is NOTHING wrong with you. These conflicting feelings are completely normal responses to any type of abuse. You are a survivor, and you are doing the best that you can. While it's normal to think like this, it probably prevented you from leaving your relationship sooner and it will probably hinder your recovery now that you have finally found the courage to leave. To fully heal and move on more positively, you have to understand one crucial and important fact: IT'S NOT YOUR FAULT. It never was, it never will be, and it's absolutely imperative that you don't allow this self-blame to play games inside of your head.

There are a lot of reasons why we blame ourselves for being abused. They are completely natural, but they are inappropriate. Once you are able to fully understand the logic behind this normal but irrational type of thinking, you can take positive steps to truly liberate yourself from this destructive self-blaming behavior. Abuse is never your fault, no matter what you do, who you are, or how you behave. Abuse is a choice made solely by the abuser. When an abuser chooses to dish out their abuse, or respond the way they do, the action of abuse or response is their responsibility and their responsibility alone. Period. No if, ands or buts.

Why Do We Believe Abuse Is Our Fault?

The simple answer is that in most cases people *abuse* because they themselves were abused in some way and learned abusive behaviors. And people who are *abused* learn a false fact from their abusers that the abuse is either normal, not that bad, ok, or worse - deserved. But the answer to that million-dollar question is actually a little more complex than that. One of the terrible things that happens to people who are abused is that it sets into motion a mental rearrangement of the way they see themselves, the person who is abusing them and the abuse they are experiencing.

A really skilled abuser will constantly reinforce the fact that they are merely *responding* to something you have said or done. If only you hadn't said what you said or done what you did, they wouldn't have been *forced* to explode or lash out at you, scream and yell, call you names or remind you how worthless you are. Over time you teach yourself that if you are good or just *perform* better, your abuser wouldn't have to "discipline" you. This creates the mindset of deserving or justified abuse which keeps you in the mental trap that your abuser has created for you. You have been groomed to be abused.

There are a number of other reasons that will cause both men and women to blame themselves for the abuse they receive. One of the things that most abusers will do is tell you that your (normal and appropriate) reaction to their abuse is wrong, bad, selfish or even worse, crazy. This aspect of abuse is called "crazy-making." Your abuser will accuse you of over-reacting and trying to be controlling--attempting to stop them from being their "authentic" self.

And heaven-forbid you make a mistake. If your abuser makes one, it's no big deal. Hey, accidents happen, it's just one of those things. Oops. But if you make one, watch out. No one could be as ignorant, worthless or thoughtless as you. As someone on an abuse blog once said, "You will just wish the Earth opened up and swallowed you. And every mistake you make will get added to "the list," logged into the ledger of irredeemable mistakes, to be held against you and remembered for eternity and brought up by them to constantly remind you of your shortcomings, forever. It's all part of the blame game. And this will make you question everything you have ever done.

Since many emotional abusers are also narcissists, they will often bully their victims into silence. If you are deeply hurt by their abusive behavior and start to get emotional, they will often say things like "God, you're so emotional or sensitive" or "Yeah, go ahead and cry your crocodile tears" or "Shut up, or I'll really give you something to cry about." This insidious behavior is designed to make you feel guilty and ashamed for having a perfectly normal and appropriate reaction to their bad behavior. The reality is that people don't cry because they are weak, they often cry because they have been strong for *way* too long.

Society can also play a role in helping us question if we are responsible for some or all of the abuse we have received. That's because sometimes the people we tell and confide in, will downplay our situation or refuse to believe us. It could be your friend, doctor, therapist, family member or a co-worker that casts doubt on your situation. And this just reinforces the idea that you might be to blame for the abusive relationship you are in.

Abuse survivors can also internalize the victim-blaming attitudes that are present in our society at large. This is a cognitive bias that most of us have and use without realizing it, called "The Just-World Hypothesis." If we see bad things happening to someone, we tend to believe that they must be happening for a reason and therefore can be attributed to something we find negative about that person, their lifestyle, behavior or choices. It is something we believe or are convinced they definitely could control.

This allows us to distance ourselves from relating to the problem or whatever happened to them. We can separate the incident from something we find problematic with the person, which allows us to say things like, "Well, I would never have done what they did" or "No wonder that happened to them" or "They kind of asked for it" or "What did they expect to happen?" But the reality is emotional abuse (or any type of abuse for that matter) can happen to anyone.

Every victim of emotional abuse needs to understand that nothing you did could ever justify the abuse you have experienced. You need to see that abuse is always about your abuser's need to have power, inflict harm and assert control. It is NEVER about what you might have "provoked" or what your abuser thinks you "deserve." Fortunately, something made you realize it was wrong and you were able to break free. But the residual effect from this type of thing is something you still need to deal with.

As you can see, there are so many different factors that encourage us to blame ourselves in an abusive relationship that it's almost inevitable we will do this. Asking yourself all of these questions is only natural, and there is nothing wrong with thinking those thoughts. But thinking like this can also be destructive, so it's important to move on from questioning or blaming yourself - to empowering yourself with knowledge. So, allow me to share a few facts with you:

1. **Abuse is *always* the fault of the abuser.** It is, has been, and always will be about your abuser's desire to establish, maintain and exert power and control over you.
2. **Abusers abuse because of *their* past, not yours.** Abuse is a learned behavior from an abusive and dysfunctional childhood, it is not a reaction to who you are as a person.
3. ***Anyone* can become a victim of emotional abuse.** All of us have vulnerabilities and situations in life that can leave us more exposed to someone trying to harm and take advantage of us.
4. **People are groomed by abusers for abuse.** Abusers are experts at grooming you to adapt and conform to their toxic behavior through repetition. They know how to wear you down.
5. **Abuse says nothing about you as a survivor.** It doesn't say anything about your character or who you are as a person. All it says is that you were in a relationship with someone who was abusive.
6. **You are *not* responsible for the abuse.** You are responsible for your reactions *to* the abuse but your reactions don't make you responsible *for* it. There is nothing you did to cause the abuse.

7. **There's nothing you could have done to change them.** No amount of patience, trying harder or doing and saying the right things can change them. Only their personal commitment to long-term professional therapy.
8. **Staying longer wouldn't have made them stop.** They can only abuse if you are available to be abused. And the more hurt you become, the less capable you are to help them anyway.
9. **Not leaving right away doesn't mean you deserve it.** There are many reasons victims can't or don't leave. It could be financial considerations, children, social or religious pressures, isolation, lack of support or fear. You are human.
10. **Your past doesn't determine your present.** Whatever has happened to you in the past, for whatever reason, does not absolve your abuser from abusing you or make you responsible for their behavior.

What you also need to understand is that the rules on the playing field are always changing. Even if you had the power to somehow address everything I just shared, and you did all of the "right" things, you wouldn't be able to stay in the game because of the constant rule changes. Let's say your spouse/partner has "trained" you to look for and immediately respond to all of their texts. They get really angry when you don't do it fast enough. So now you text them randomly throughout the day to say hello and make them feel important, only now they accuse you of checking up on *them*.

If you are hanging out with friends and God-forbid you happen to have a conversation with someone of the opposite sex to be friendly, they will later accuse you of flirting. If they are telling a story and you join them and try to add something to the story, they will tell you not to interrupt them and accuse you of being rude. So now you don't say anything at family gatherings or at get-togethers with friends. You don't speak unless you are spoken to. They then accuse you of making them look bad because you are not interacting with anyone.

Let's say they hate when you talk on the phone or text with your friends or family. They will hover over you, demand your calls are all on speaker phone and listen intently to your conversation. They may roll their eyes or make faces at you during the conversations. When you are done they will claim that you are being disrespectful to them and taking "together" time away from them. So now when you get a call or text, you don't respond and just set the phone down. But this makes them suspicious, and they ask you why you didn't take the call or answer the text. This will escalate to the point that they may believe you are having an affair or are doing something behind their back. So now you turn off your phone completely when you around them so they won't get upset, and then they ask you why you never get any calls or texts anymore.

Do you see how crazy and pointless this is? EVERYTHING you do is a potential trigger for them. Every move can subliminally make them think that you still have your own life and are not completely under their power and control. They don't understand that every abusive action of theirs causes a reaction in you (even with the best intentions of trying to make them happy), and every action they take will most likely contradict another they take later.

They continually act out in the moment, in the hopes of controlling the environment so that they can control their fears, mistrust, and insecurities. They are in a perpetual state of being tormented by their own emotions. And there's nothing you can do to help them or fix it. This is how hard it is to deal with emotional abuse, and how pointless it is to even try.

Steps for Self-Reflection

It is imperative that you understand how important it is to not only liberate yourself from this type of environment but also the effects your abuser's behavior has had on your way of thinking. This requires that you open your eyes and force yourself to see how they have truly treated you. Here are some questions to ask yourself:

- How would you feel if this type of abuse happened to one of your children?
- Would it be acceptable to you, or would it trigger any form of rage inside of you?
- How do or how would your family and friends feel about this behavior? Would they put up with it?
- Looking at it from the outside now, how does behavior like this make you feel?
- Are there qualities or traits about you that might have led you to be too compassionate toward your abuser and tolerant of their behavior?
- Do you perhaps have too much empathy for your abuser which allowed you to keep feeling sorry for them?
- Do you have a rescuer mentality that perhaps caused you to overlook warning signs that showed themselves already early in the relationship?
- How do you feel about the fact that your abuser deliberately caused you to become confused and vulnerable so they could manipulate, dominate, and blame you?
- Do you better understand things like splitting behavior, gaslighting, blame shifting and the silent treatment?

Here are some things you can do to help you in your healing and recovery efforts:

- Make a list of all of the toxic behaviors you will no longer tolerate from anyone, especially in any relationship going forward. (This in itself is liberating and empowering.)
- Make a list of the things you are discovering about yourself.
- Make a list of the things you value in life and others.
- What do you now value about yourself?

- What are your strong points and attributes?
- What are you most proud of in life?
- What are the changes you want or need to make going forward?

Do you realize you survived the worst behavior anyone could possibly tolerate? Do you realize how strong that makes you? There's a great quote by trauma recovery specialist Michelle Rosenthall that sums up the beginning of the recovery process perfectly: "Trauma creates change you don't choose. Healing is about creating change you do choose."

As you start to move forward, just remember, abuse of any kind is never your fault, and it certainly is never justified. Remove yourself from the situation you have just been through and ask yourself this: Why would anyone ever deserve to be abused? How could any person think that abusing another person is justified? No normal, sane, empathetic human being would ever think like that. And neither should you. You are an amazing human being, created in the image of God, and worthy of only the best treatment from others, especially in a close and intimate relationship with someone who claims to love you.

Healing from emotional abuse isn't easy to do, and it will take time. It took time for you to get sucked into an abusive relationship, so it stands to reason it will take some time, effort and patience to recover from it. But the greater the distance grows from when you were abused, the stronger and more resilient you will become and you will gain tremendous insight that you didn't have before. And knowing, understanding and believing that the abuse you encountered and were subjected to wasn't your fault, is an important step in your recovery.

5

Regaining Your Lost Identity

Our personal identity is one of the most important things to understand about ourselves. It consists of a group of attributes, qualities and values that not only defines how we view ourselves but also how we think other people see us. Knowing who we are and what makes us tick is essential because it truly affects everything else about us. How we see ourselves has an impact on how we look at life, the roles we undertake, the things we participate in, the projects and activities we complete, how we handle conflicts and even whom we choose as friends. Our identity also helps us connect to others and gives us a sense of who we are.

We can sometimes experience a loss of identity when there is a major change in our life such as a career change, job loss, a child going to college, the loss of a role that once defined us, the loss of a friend or someone we dearly love. This loss of identity can result in increased levels of anxiety, depression, low self-esteem, a feeling of isolation, a loss of self-confidence and chronic loneliness. This often leaves a gap or empty space inside of us that can leave us vulnerable to outside influences.

We can also lose some of our identity when we gradually merge with someone in a relationship or marriage. If it's healthy, then it should be reciprocal in encouraging and maintaining an individual sense of self for both partners or spouses. Over time, as the relationship deepens, we may lose some of our sense of self, as we accommodate, adjust our behaviors, and support the person we love. There may be some change in our level of independence, as a small level of healthy co-dependency can strengthen the relationship. But that's the whole point of two people merging into one. It's a desire to care for each other that normally attracts two people to each other in the first place.

But it's not that way in a toxic, unhealthy, abusive relationship. One of the truly unfortunate and almost unavoidable side effects that come out of being emotionally and mentally abused by someone, is that those who are on the receiving end of the abuse can often lose their sense of identity in the relationship. It can be a fairly lengthy process that takes place over a period of time, or it can happen quite suddenly following a major event or trauma in the relationship. But no matter the length of time it takes, an abusive partner will eventually and completely wipe out their partner's independence, resulting in a total loss of who they are.

And this is made worse by the fact that as we lose our identity and sense of self, we are likely to seek our sense of self-worth even more from our abuser. It suddenly becomes very important how they view us, as our sense of value and self-worth become more dependent on external factors such as our physical appearance, our abuser's approval and the success of the relationship. And the more isolated we become from others, the more dependent we become on our abuser to make us feel good about ourselves. And sadly, the more we seek praise and reassurance from them, the less we get and the more we are put down.

But in reality, our emotional well-being should ultimately depend on how we feel about ourselves, not on how our abuser feels about us or the validation of others. That new dependency on external validation from our abuser also prevents the real "us" from blossoming, which impacts our personal growth and sense of dignity, as well as our opportunity for happiness.

The problem is that in an emotionally abusive relationship, your abuser will do everything they can to remove every opinion, viewpoint, and personal thought you have until you've reached a complete loss of who you are. You in essence, become an extension of them. And that is their goal. After all, it becomes much easier to control a person when they have no thoughts, opinions, or feelings of their own. The abuser wants to achieve a total loss of identity in their intended target. And this type of treatment and manipulation is often referred to as perspecticide.

This term is credited to Evan Stark, an award-winning researcher and professor at Rutgers University, who first coined the term in his 2007 book, *Coercive Control*. In its simplest form, perspecticide is the incapacity to know what you know, as a result of a person's abuse. With perspecticide, your abuser will slowly chip away at your perspective until you have no thoughts of your own. And at that point, you will no longer have your own personal identity.

To help you understand just how truly evil perspecticide is, you need to know that it was first used as a psychological manipulation tactic on prisoners of war and later has been incorporated as a tactic used by cult leaders to control other's thinking. In fact, many victims often compare living with an abuser (especially a narcissist) to living in a cult, only with even more isolation because you are totally alone.

The problem is, most survivors of abuse aren't able to grasp the magnitude of their identity loss until they have left their abuser for good. That's because an abuser's control over their partner/spouse is exceptionally subtle, yet so severe and deeply embedded in the mind of their target, that they often struggle to manage their life on their own, even after they begin to recover.

My own personal loss of identity happened after I lost my first wife, the love of my life to cancer. I was very sad, lonely and confused, and I was questioning who I was and wanted to be going forward. And this made me extremely vulnerable. I think it's fair to say I was still discovering my new identity when I dove headfirst into my emotionally abusive relationship with someone who suffered from all four of the Cluster B personality disorders. She made it easy for me to tie my identity to hers. Initially, she showered me with so much love, affection and validation, that it was almost overwhelming. She became my rescuer at a time when I desperately wanted to be needed. And then the bottom fell out.

I wasn't sure who I was or what I wanted out of life anymore at the point I met my abuser, so it was easy for me to focus all of my attention on her needs (demands), and boy did she have a ton of them. Over time, I basically convinced myself that her needs and desires were more important than mine. I bought into the idea that our relationship was all about her and not about us.

At that point the real, true me ceased to exist anymore. All I wanted to do was please her and make her the happiest she had ever been in her life. And she had plenty of suggestions which slowly turned into demands and requirements and then devolved into continuous put downs and insults when I couldn't possibly live up to her ever-expanding expectations. And this happened over a number of months and then years. What started out as subtle put-downs and negative thought-planting eventually turned into full-blown psychological abuse.

Looking back, it's easy for me to see how her abuse tactics were so effective at causing me to lose my own identity. She elevated gaslighting, manipulation, constant criticism and the silent treatment to an art form, in order to confuse me and break down my self-perceptions, which in turn made me more dependent on her for the "truth" about who I was. She was an expert at convincing me that everything she told me was in my "best interest" and for my "benefit." And it becomes very difficult to prevent the loss of your identity when your abuser is constantly undermining and deceiving you.

Being in an emotionally abusive relationship changed me permanently. I thought I could compromise everything about myself to be with this beautiful woman because I didn't feel whole without her. For me, the relationship came first, before my interests, my friends, my family, and even myself. And of course, she took advantage of my mindset to shape and mold me into her perfectly obedient "partner." I became confused and found I couldn't trust my instincts. There was a point in the relationship when I truly thought I might be going crazy.

I allowed myself to be devalued, ignored, belittled and insulted by her. I became a victim and lost my personal identity, until I was able to finally re-find myself just before I found the strength to walk away from her and end the relationship. It took me a while to shed the victim mindset, rediscover my inner strength, and with it, my personal identity. I feel pretty good about myself again and I am truly happy with what is taking place in my life. I can look back now without feeling too much pain, but to this day I still can't tell you who I was during that time, and perhaps I never will.

And of course, this isn't remotely how a healthy relationship should be. Your relationship should amplify your best qualities and feed into your identity without your partner feeling threatened. By their very nature, all deep relationships require some emotional give and take. You give parts of your personality to your partner while absorbing some of theirs. While it is perfectly normal to experience a small loss of self-identity as you merge and grow into a couple, it should not require a loss of personal identity and independence from either partner.

It's not easy to notice a loss of self-identity as its happening because most emotional abusers are incredibly subtle and adept at making it happen. And even if you are going into the relationship without a super strong sense of self, your abuser will notice it immediately and use it to their advantage. They go into every relationship with just one end goal in mind, complete control over you. They don't want you to think for yourself, only about them. And they have a number of different ways for achieving their goal.

The Erosion of Your Identity

Most abusers will share horrible stories about their dysfunctional childhood, past abuse and toxic family members and former lovers. You probably had tremendous empathy for them and told yourself that they just needed someone to understand and support them and show them compassion. That's when you made the decision to invest your time, energy, and self into fulfilling their needs and desires. But you soon found out that it's not enough. It's never enough. So, you reevaluate and try even harder. You pour yourself into them.

Then they will start to drop little hints like, "If you only did this or that" or "If you were only like this" they could be happy and everything would be perfect. So, you try harder to please them. Then they start to actually point out your flaws (according to them). First, it's the things you say and do, and then the way you look. You will feel like they are analyzing everything you say and do which will lead you to question every aspect about yourself. Then they will suddenly compare you unfavorably to all of their former lovers in every aspect of your relationship.

Now when you state an opinion, they will tell you that you are wrong, mistaken or worse. They will try to make you feel like a village idiot. In fact, the mere fact that you still have an opinion on something will offend your abuser. And of course, this will lead you to not only question your thoughts, but eventually believe that your thoughts are wrong and then you will feel guilty for sharing them.

Then your abuser will attack your past, your friends, family and anything that happened to you and/or anyone in your life before them. They will basically try to minimize your prior accomplishments and devalue everything you have ever done or hold dear in life. Your past successes will just be because of luck and good fortune, and any failures will be because of flaws they have already pointed out in you. After a while you will just stop talking about anything that happened to you before you met them or anyone else in your life. And that's the whole idea. They want all your focus to be on them.

Finally, they will implement an array of gaslighting techniques on you to the point you believe you can't find or remember anything and that you lose and forget everything. At that point you will truly believe you are going crazy and you won't have any idea of who you are or what has happened to you. At that point, they will have achieved utter and total control over you.

They will make you feel so worthless that you will come to believe that you must listen to your abuser for guidance. And in between all of this, they will manage to compel themselves to show you just enough artificial attention and brief moments of love to keep you from even remotely considering leaving them. At this point you will start to get depressed and feel completely isolated. You have given up complete control of yourself and are now strictly in survival mode. You now exist only for them.

A total loss of identity doesn't happen overnight. But over time, an emotional abuser gradually implements these tactics to slowly chip away at both your perception of self and the world around you. There are a number of identity crisis symptoms that can help you identify if you were exposed to and are suffering perspecticide from the actions of your emotional abuser. Understanding how the identity crisis symptoms affect you and how your abuser used them against you to their advantage are the first steps in recovering your identity and helping you in your overall abuse recovery.

1. You don't recognize the person you have become and you have a hard time remembering your former self.
2. You feel ashamed of who you have become, and you don't think of yourself as changed but rather and literally, a completely different person.
3. You struggle to talk about yourself to other people especially around your abuser. You feel like a complete failure and that you don't have anything worth sharing.
4. You go along with everything your abuser suggests or demands and you become afraid to share an alternative thought or opinion because of how they might respond to you.
5. Before making any decision, you wonder what your abuser would say or want you to say.
6. You feel like your life lacks or has lost its purpose, and you have no sense of motivation.
7. You believe you don't need or deserve to have anything in life, and you feel guilty when there is something you desire or want to get for yourself.
8. You don't feel comfortable about anything you do. You doubt yourself and every decision you make. You question your ability to please your abuser.
9. You pay more attention to your appearance because your abuser points out all of your flaws.
10. You feel uncomfortable when you are away from your abuser because you don't know how they will treat you when you return.
11. You've hit a plateau in life, and everything requires a lot of effort. You feel like you're living on autopilot and you have become a passive bystander in your own life.
12. You find that you don't know what to do when you're alone. You spend all of your spare time cleaning, buying cards, gifts, flowers or thinking of things to do to make your abuser happy.

Healing from Identity Loss

Many survivors of emotional abuse don't even realize that they're suffering from a loss of self-identity until they have left the relationship and often aren't sure what to do with themselves because their inner sense of identity has vanished. Awareness that you have 'lost' your identity is one of the first steps toward finding it again.

A good counselor or therapist can help you explore who you are, what has made you into 'you', define your own qualities and attributes, and remove the need to rely on the external validation of others. This can help you to lose all those negative labels that your abuser hung around your neck, and bring out your true identity again.

Crafting our self-identity is a life-long, ongoing process that most people don't give much concrete thought to, it just kind of happens. We slowly build our interests, hopes and dreams. We learn things, take jobs, go down career paths, pick up hobbies and experience different activities. This all shapes who we are, what we believe, and how we express ourselves. It takes time for our identity to form and then it constantly reshapes itself. So please be patient with yourself and realize it will take time to get your sense of identity back.

Healing from identity loss is a long road, but don't be afraid to travel down it. You deserve to have your own thoughts, feelings, and emotions again. You may be feeling a lot of resentment and anger right now, (and rightfully so) especially toward your abuser, but you *can* move forward.

It might look like a difficult or even impossible journey right now, and your identity will probably look different from what it was before (if you can even remember it), but you'll come out at the end of the process stronger, more assertive, and with a better perception of yourself than you ever had before. Here are some tips to help you on your journey to healing and recovering your identity:

- **Surround yourself with supportive people.** Reconnect with the friends and family members your abuser forced you to push away. Most of them will understand and most will validate your experience. Observe and appreciate all of their positive personality traits with a new set of eyes.

- **Do something your abuser didn't want to do or always said you couldn't.** This could be a hobby, career, or something you've always wanted to experience. Perhaps it's a place you've always wanted to travel to. Do something just because *you* want to do it.

- **Move slowly.** You may have a hard time communicating with other people and making decisions for yourself in the beginning. It may take time to get your sea legs back. It's okay to not know everything about yourself yet. This is all part of healing from identity loss.

- **Beware of your motivations.** You can leave a toxic relationship and the abuser that made it that way, but if you don't heal what attracted you to them, you will meet them again. The same demon, just in a different person. If you move too fast, you might end up in another toxic situation or wind up turning to unhealthy coping tools.

- **Set boundaries and stand your ground.** There are plenty of Cluster Bs and other abusive people out there. It's important to know where your boundaries lie and stick to them. Where will you draw the line between a future healthy relationship and loss of self-identity?

- **Cut off ALL ties to your former abuser.** An emotional abuser will use any opportunity to keep you in their web and make your life miserable. Block them on your phone, social media and emails, change your personal passwords, remove them from any joint accounts. Do NOT give them any opportunity to stay in your life.

When you finally escape from your abusive partner and go no contact, you might feel a little uncomfortable. Your abuser manipulated you into depending upon their approval, feelings, and well-being for so long that healing your self-image may feel selfish and unnatural. It's not. Embrace the process, liberate yourself and look forward to the new you!

Understand that you are a child of God and made in His image. Psalm 139:13-14 says

> *"For you created my inmost being; you knit me together in my mother's womb. I praise you because I am fearfully and wonderfully made; your works are wonderful; I know that full well."*

Genesis 1:27 says

> *"So God created man in his own image, in the image of God he created him; male and female he created them."*

What this means is that you are really special to God. You were lovingly made in His image because He loves you deeply. You are a part of His innermost being. And the best thing of all is that when we turn toward God and make him the Lord of our life, he will to continue to shape and transform us. 2 Corinthians 3:18 says that we

> *"All reflect God's glory and are being transformed into his likeness with ever increasing glory."*

Every single human being, no matter how much the image of God in them is marred by sin, illness, weakness, age, disability or abuse, still has the status of being made in God's image and therefore must be treated with the dignity and respect that is due to God's image-bearer. But it gets even better because the Bible tells us in one verse earlier that

> *"Where the Spirit of the Lord is, there is freedom."*

That's right, freedom. Freedom to leave our abuser and run into the open arms of an all-loving God.

6

The Effects of Emotional Abuse

In addition to losing your personal identity, emotional abuse can leave you with several long-term and short-term side effects. These might be physical such as stomach pains, indigestion, nausea, headaches, excess sweating (hyperhidrosis), muscle tension, a racing heartbeat, tremors and fatigue. The side effects might also be psychological and emotional such as anxiety, depression, moodiness, difficulty concentrating, chronic fear, sleep disorders, nervous breakdown or Post Traumatic Stress Disorder (PTSD). I want to highlight the four most severe of these.

Anxiety Disorder

Everyone experiences fear and anxiety from time to time, mostly in response to specific situations. However, someone with uncontrollable and irrational worry that persists may have a generalized anxiety disorder (GAD). People with generalized anxiety disorder worry excessively about the outcome of events. They suffer from restlessness, lose focus and often have difficulty concentrating. They can become indecisive. They become anxious and worrisome and often experience fatigue, irritability, headaches and moments when they struggle to breathe properly without physical exertion.

Depression

People suffering from depression often experience a persistent feeling of worthlessness and low self-esteem. They can feel excessive guilt for things they have or haven't done, often dwelling on past actions to an unhealthy extent. People with depression often remove themselves from otherwise happy, healthy relationships, and struggle to form new connections with others. They can often feel like a burden to those who care about them, or may simply be too exhausted and over-whelmed to deal with more social interaction.

One of the more common symptoms of depression is fatigue, lethargy, and constant tiredness. And this can be tied to a significant change in sleep patterns and changes in appetite. Anger and irritability are a common symptom of depression and anxiety, along with persistent physical symptoms, sadness and trouble concentrating.

One of the most serious symptoms of depression, can be suicidal ideation, which can take the form of persistent suicidal thoughts or even plans to commit suicide. If you're experiencing symptoms of suicidal ideation, be sure to get in touch with a mental health professional right away. You can also reach out to the National Suicide Prevention Hotline online, or call them at 1-800-273-8255.

Nervous Breakdown

For some people, emotional abuse eventually leads to nervous break-down. While there is no clinical definition for this phenomenon, it typically refers to the point at which psychological distress disrupts functionality. This loss of function occurs when the effects of emotional abuse become too much to bear. A person might begin to feel more on edge, find it more difficult to sleep and find themselves thinking more negatively about themselves. They may also feel increasingly hopeless and incompetent in what they are doing. Then one day they wake up and perhaps they just can't face going to work, or getting out of bed.

The breakdown occurs when the stress and distress are not dealt with and they build up to the point of the mind breaking down.

The exact features of nervous breakdown may vary from person to person, but usually involves losing the ability or desire to participate in social and professional activities as well as a diminished desire to self-care (including eating and personal hygiene). In addition to feelings of depression and anxiety, you may experience many of the other side effects of emotional abuse mentioned earlier. Sometimes, you may simply cease to feel anything at all.

Nervous breakdowns do not necessarily occur while you are in the abusive relationship. In fact, it is common for survivors to experience nervous breakdown only after the relationship has ended, sometimes months or even years later, especially if you have never had the opportunity to process your experiences in a healthy way.

Post-Traumatic Stress Disorder (PTSD)

This is an anxiety disorder that comes with difficult symptoms that interfere with everyday life. Some of these symptoms involve remembering or avoiding trauma associated with the cause of the person's (PTSD). This disorder comes with other symptoms as well, such as anxiety, nervousness, and negative thoughts.

(PTSD) is commonly associated with physical sources of trauma, such as war, physical assault, or sexual assault. But mental health experts have come to realize that mental and emotional abuse can lead to PTSD as well. All PTSD, even from physical forms of trauma, is based on emotional and psychological reactions to trauma, which develop because of fear and distress. It can also be from any event(s) the person finds disturbing or distressing.

Mental and emotional abuse in any close relationship or marriage may make a person feel as though they are worthless or do not deserve better, even after they leave the relationship. It may also lead them toward other unhealthful thoughts. There may still be lingering thoughts and feelings of confusion, guilt, shame, hopelessness, loneliness, and low self-esteem. The longer you were in the relationship and exposed to the abuse, the more prolonged these side effects can be. You may also have difficulty trusting anyone again for quite some time, especially in a new relationship after you have been put through the ringer by an abusive Cluster B.

Bargaining

One of the other effects of abuse is that in the beginning of recovery, many survivors are not able to clearly assess their situation, and look at it through the lenses of reality. That's because they have become trained to look at it through the lenses provided by their abuser. This causes the person who was abused to question their own emotions rather than the behavior of the abuser. It allows them to bargain with themselves in order to downplay the pain they are feeling. You might think "You know it really wasn't that bad" or "It could have been worse" or "If only I had or hadn't done this than perhaps they wouldn't have ... etc."

Bargaining is a subconscious way of not dealing with the pain caused from the abuse to its deepest extent. It's somewhat like a softer form of denial. It's like you're trying to convince your brain "If I don't see it as being so bad, it won't hurt so bad." In this way, bargaining becomes one of the coping mechanisms we try to use when trying to come to terms with the difficult reality of the situation we were just in and then finally reach a point of acceptance.

Acceptance would be saying, "Okay, I've got a clear picture of what happened to me. It was wrong, it's not my fault and I was right to get out of the relationship and leave my abuser." Acceptance is when you look back and see every abusive pebble and rock that was thrown at you, and understand how they combined to create a landslide of toxic waste that tore your life apart and left you a shattered mess of brokenness.

Bargaining is often thought of as a stage of grief, though most abuse recovery experts now think that grief does not happen in "stages," but rather some of the "stages" may happen, and others may not, and when they do happen, they do not always happen in any specific order.

When you have suffered from emotional abuse for a significant amount of time, you will often still feel bad after you have left the relationship. It may feel like there is a void inside of you which creates unhappiness and brings about feelings of anger, betrayal, sadness and a sense of loss. No matter how you experienced it, the aftermath of emotional abuse can be overwhelming. It feels awful because it is, *not* because there is something wrong with you. It will get better and you will eventually regain your sense of self again.

7

Understanding Emotional Abuse Trauma

The pain one can feel from the emotional abuse dished out by a Cluster B, runs deep and can often cause as much, if not more trauma than physical wounds can. I'm not minimizing the wounds inflicted from physical abuse, because it is horrible and often leaves visible scars. It's just that most physical wounds will eventually heal, while emotional trauma can stay with you for quite some time and leaves its own invisible scars. It can have an impact on who you are as a person, and it can affect the way you think and the ability to process emotions and heal. The more abuse you are exposed to, the greater impact it can have on you, and the longer it can take to recover from those wounds and become healthy again.

Whether you realize it or not, the trauma you may be experiencing from covert emotional and psychological abuse has most likely caused long-lasting effects on your body and your brain. In order to heal from abuse, it's important to understand how it has affected your thoughts, feelings, healing, and everyday responses to life.

According to research from the New York University Medical Center, chronic stress resulting from emotional abuse or any other kind of trauma releases cortisol, a stress hormone which can damage and affect the growth of the hippocampus, the main area of the brain associated with learning and memory. This can lead to mental diagnoses like depression, anxiety disorder and PTSD.

Defining Trauma

Trauma is defined as coming from an injury, severe mental and emotional stress or a serious or ongoing threat that overwhelms your body and the brain's ability to cope. And make no mistake about it, living with a Cluster B emotional abuser can create *severe* trauma. All of the non-stop anger, devaluing, blame shifting, gaslighting, name-calling, lies, yelling, manipulation, betrayal and humiliation is beyond anyone's ability to cope. And the problem is, the effects of the trauma don't end when you leave the abuse. Sadly, there's an imprint that the abuse leaves on one's brain and body, and it can affect you going forward.

To make matters worse, you can often experience blame shifting after you leave your abuser. Just when you think you have finally stopped being blamed for your reactions, responses and struggles by your abuser, well-meaning friends and family members can often continue the behavior. They can often question what you have gone through and why you "tolerated" the abuse.

This is often brought on by their own lack of understanding of abuse or the personal wounds they feel from you having disassociated from them because of your abuser's behaviors or demands. They will often end up blaming victims for staying with their abuser longer than they deem appropriate. Trauma can affect us so negatively that we often end up blaming ourselves too, and that should never happen.

The terrible abuse one is exposed to from someone who suffers from Cluster B personality disorders can change you from a peaceful, empathetic and compassionate person into a nervous, anxious, panicked, confused, self-doubting mess. But let me make this perfectly clear from the very beginning, you aren't crazy, weak, stupid, unstable or anything else you may have been told by your abuser or anyone else. You are actually brave for leaving your abuser, strong for your ability to withstand the abuse and exceptionally resilient because you are going to heal from the trauma you have experienced. You are a survivor!

Because emotional abuse comes in so many forms and is delivered in so many different ways, our brain and body have a way of storing the experiences, memories and sensations, even if we can't or don't consciously remember them all ourselves. Sometimes we can "zone out" during an onslaught of abuse or even block out the moment completely.

This is because abuse creates changes in the region of our brain (the somatosensory cortex) that receives and processes sensory information and perceptions from different parts of our body such as touch, temperature and pain. This means that there is always an emotional element from the abuse that remains with us regardless of whether or not we remember every specific detail or completely block it out.

Our Built-In Defense Mechanism

The good thing about this is that we have a built-in defense mechanism for dealing with things we may not be able to emotionally handle at the time they happen. The bad thing about this is that sometimes our inability to experience the feelings from the abuse we have encountered in a healthy way leaves us susceptible to either delayed anger or emotional outbursts when those blocked out experiences are finally discovered and processed, or dulled responses to them because we have become emotionally "numb" from the experience. So, survivors of abuse are often caught between our brain's unique capability for self-preservation during the abuse, and its ability to interfere with our healing from it afterward.

If we can't take action to stop the abuse when it is happening, or we can't get away from it, the body keeps activating these survival responses. They continue long after an event has passed. And when we have to live with abuse, these body systems get activated too often and too strongly.

Our stress hormones, brain circuits and nervous system go on high alert or operate on overload and the longer the abuse continues, the more sensitive our system gets, and eventually it gets stuck in that high alert/overload mode. What is really sad is that trauma robs you of the feeling that you are in charge of yourself. It can leave you feeling anxious, depressed, overwhelmed, lost, hopeless, and disconnected from the rest of the world.

Because of the trauma from the abuse, survivors often experience the world through clouded eyes, with new unwelcome feelings and emotions and a changed nervous system. After each subsequent emotional trigger we experience, we take longer to return to our old baseline of normal, healthy feelings. And with each incident, the stress becomes harder and harder to handle. This can leave us dealing with many new triggers and a feeling of not having control of our thoughts and feelings. And this in turn can lead to difficulty with problem-solving, concentration, memory, organization, decision-making, motivation, and emotional regulation.

The Healing Process

Healing from emotional abuse involves learning how to turn off the alarms we feel from the triggers and allowing the calming influence of our parasympathetic system (which controls our heart rate) to take control again. This allows our brain to properly process experiences and information so we can distinguish between what is important and relevant, and what is not. And this helps us draw proper conclusions about what we are experiencing. It gives us the ability to once again sort through our feelings, make decisions, change and control our thoughts, and see options for how we can live life. It allows us to re-experience the feelings and sensations we like such as love, joy, imagination, pleasure and happiness.

Anytime emotional abuse is inflicted on us, our brain attempts to protect itself by re-routing abundant levels of stress and pain to avoid an overload. And this is what can interfere with our ability to have a healthy response to the abuse, even months or years after the threat or traumatic situation is gone. Fortunately, our brains are resilient, and with the right support, counseling and/or therapy we can repair the damage and recover from it. New coping skills can be learned, bad memories can be dealt with, and our hearts can be repaired so we can once again experience life to its full potential.

What Are the Signs of Emotional Abuse Trauma?

Mental and emotional abuse can take a serious toll on anyone who has been on the receiving end of it. The trauma that comes from the abuse can look many different ways, because the abuse can alter your sense of confidence, safety, security, trust and self-worth. You may lack energy, motivation or interest to do even the most basic or normal things you need to do in order to take care of yourself and function properly. We all respond to trauma in different ways, and while there are no "right" or "wrong" ways to come to terms with significant events, there are definitely some common trauma signs and symptoms to be aware of. Emotional and mental abuse trauma symptoms include:

- Denial or shock
- Lack of memory
- Anger, irritability and mood fluctuations
- Fear, anxiety and excessive worrying
- Feelings of sadness or hopelessness
- Confusion and second guessing yourself
- Lack of focus and difficulty staying on task
- Heightened sense of danger and alertness
- Difficulty building connections with others
- Feeling withdrawn and disconnected from people and life

- Denying the impact or extent of an abusive event or that it even happened
- Feeling overwhelmed by life
- Spacing out and forgetting things
- Feeling unsafe even after you are out of the abuse
- You are emotional, sad and constantly cry
- You have low or no motivation
- Have a hard time thinking or concentrating
- You are easily triggered by events or conversations
- You feel negative about everything
- You have a hard time making decisions or reaching conclusions
- You don't trust yourself or your feelings
- You are isolating yourself from others
- Feeling empty, helpless, trapped or weighed down
- You've lost your sense of purpose and direction
- You feel worthless, like a nobody
- You struggle to forgive yourself, others or your abuser
- You feel lost or disconnected from the world, others and God

Trauma not only affects our mental health but it can also disrupt our physical health as well. Some of the physical effects of trauma include:

- Fatigue and low energy
- Lack of self-care
- Nightmares
- Disordered eating
- Elevated or racing heartbeat
- Muscle tension
- Aches and pains
- Being startled easily
- Chronic illness
- Feeling withdrawn and disconnected from people and life
- Engaging in risky behaviors or addictions
- Constant feeling of exhaustion

- Constant headaches or indigestion
- You just don't feel like yourself
- Insomnia, restless sleep or unusual sleep patterns

In many cases, the signs and triggers of trauma are often connected with exposure to sights, sounds or experiences that may remind you of your abuser or specific events in your abusive relationship. The trauma can be divided into three categories: acute trauma, chronic trauma and complex trauma.

- **Acute trauma** is most often associated with a single specific event. It can come from being a victim of an act of violence by your abuser, theft of money or something dear they took from you or anything they did that might have disrupted or made you doubt your sense of safety and security. This type of trauma is often connected to post-traumatic stress disorder.
- **Chronic trauma** is associated with events that happen or abuse tactics that your abuser uses against you over and over again, such as shouting, constant questioning, belittling or insulting you. While reactions to acute trauma are often immediate, reactions to chronic trauma may not be apparent for months or even years.
- **Complex trauma** is similar to chronic trauma in that the events are recurring. However, with complex trauma, the events happened through actions or inactions of someone that you should have been able to trust. Someone who experiences ongoing abuse, profound neglect or severe gaslighting by their spouse or partner will often experience trauma traits, even after they have left the relationship.

Diagnosing Trauma

While there are a number of surveys and questionnaires that are designed to help you assess yourself for trauma, I would caution against solely relying on them. If you can identify with more than a couple of the listed symptoms above, I would strongly recommend working with a licensed counselor/therapist to help you discover and recover from the damage done by your abuser. A skilled counselor/therapist can also help you understand how traumatic events in your relationship life may impact the way you see the world going forward, and they can help you be proactive in addressing the trauma you have experienced.

In addition to counseling and therapy, art, exercise, music, prayer and meditation; a supportive church and the companionship, conversation and loving support of friends and family can provide you with tremendous forms of self-care to help you restore the health of your mind and body. Remember that the abuse you endured took a while to negatively impact your mind and body, so it will probably take a while for you to recover. Just give yourself time, but stick with it and soon you will start to feel good again.

8

Working Through the Grief

One of the most important aspects of abuse recovery that often doesn't get enough attention is the honest reality of the grief one feels after leaving the relationship. This may sound absolutely ridiculous to someone who has never been in a toxic and abusive relationship. After all, you finally saw things clearly and found the strength to leave your abuser so now you should be kicking up your heels and celebrating right? How could you possibly miss what you walked away from?

The reality is quite a bit more complicated than that. Just because someone hurt you and caused you an incredible amount of pain doesn't mean you won't miss them. The loss of a bad relationship and the spouse or partner who you were deeply in love with is still a loss. Your relationship once had a beginning that was probably quite magnetic, causing you to fall deeply in love and draw quite close to your abuser. But now you have the difficult task of recognizing the relationship is over and has an ending—one you reluctantly chose to initiate, but one you were not prepared for nevertheless.

When we enter into a romantic relationship or marriage, we usually do so with the hope and dreams of a beautiful and life-long future together. When we experience those beautiful moments with our spouse or partner, we experience the confirmation of this future hope or expectation coming to a reality. Once we experience abuse, rejection and distancing, we start to fear we will lose that romantic dream. And this fear of loss is what often allows us to accept our abuser's affection and reconciliation after each abusive episode. We are looking for a sign that our hopes and dreams will be restored.

When the abusive relationship does come to an end, it is not just the abusive, painful moments that come to an end, it is also the loss of the loving, caring and romantic moments. We aren't just grieving the loss of the good times; we are also grieving the loss that our hopes and dreams for the relationship are not going to be realized. And this complicates our grief when we choose to leave our emotional abuser.

In my case, I invested close to four years of intense love, affection, effort, energy, grace, time and emotion with the all-consuming task of trying to somehow please my emotional abuser. And there were definitely brief moments that were good and tender. At least they felt that way to me. But along with the constant anger, rage and hate directed my way, I also saw someone who was dysfunctional and deeply wounded inside, which made me feel a tremendous amount of empathy toward her at times. Unfortunately, she never owned her behavior or took responsibility for it. She made no real attempt or effort to get help for her Cluster B disorders, and that also left me with the feeling of "Oh, what could have been if only she had ... etc."

What I have discovered is that with this type of "loss" comes a number of conflicting emotions, and a never-ending and exhausting kind of grief. I was not remotely prepared for the full extent of self-reckoning that I would encounter and have to deal with once I finally found the strength to leave her. I wasn't surprised by how emotional I was the first few days after I left. In fact, I pretty much expected it. But I never imagined that it would only be the beginning of an emotional roller coaster I would have to struggle and deal with for many months. And that was *with* the help of an amazing counselor. I can't even begin to imagine what that journey would have been like without him to help me work through the emotional challenges I encountered along the way.

Acknowledging the End of the Relationship

It is important to recognize that when any relationship ends, even a toxic relationship; your body, mind and heart will probably experience a range of feelings. Some survivors will be tempted to just try to move on from the relationship. But this can often prevent you from fully coming to terms with everything you have experienced, learning from it and moving forward in a way that's healthy and positive. You are experiencing a loss that is painful and a process of grief that will often have a mind of its own.

It's perfectly okay to have conflicting feelings throughout the day. You may feel an intense amount of sadness one minute, calming relief another, or raging anger and frustration followed by pure happiness the next, but they all serve a purpose. Be patient with yourself and embrace each feeling you are going through. They are often fleeting and temporary, so ride them out and know they will pass. When we accept the grieving process we are able to recognize and value our fluctuating feelings. Your feelings are real, and you are experiencing them for a reason.

One of the things I have learned is that the different stages and feelings of grief are cyclical. They are not the same all of the time. Moments of feeling like you are making progress and healing, are often followed by moments of confusion and frustration when you feel like you just took a step back. It happens, and is true of all types of grief. But it is very important to understand that this will happen when you're grieving an emotionally abusive relationship.

After all, the type of abuse you experienced was *emotional*. It came from someone you trusted, deeply loved and cared about. They attacked and affected the very core of your being. You will probably go through moments of anger, anxiety, denial, bargaining, depression and ultimately acceptance, but you will experience them, probably several times a day, every day.

Over time these stages will spread farther apart which is a relief. But you will be really confused when you have a good week, and then a good month only to suddenly find yourself crying in your car because something triggered that emotion deep in the recess of your mind and you won't know why.

The other day I was sitting in the stands at a soccer game and truly enjoying myself. Our local team is really good this year and playing some exciting ball. They had just scored a goal and I was celebrating along with everyone else. I sat back down and all of a sudden out of nowhere I just started to cry. Tears were streaming down my face as I started to notice all of the couples, families and friends celebrating together. And the loneliness of my situation hit me. I guess I just needed to grieve. After a couple of minutes, the feeling went away and I was able to thoroughly enjoy the rest of the game. It was just a momentary wave of grief. And that's often the way grief works. It comes in waves.

Over the past two years I have become pretty adept at knowing when a wave of grief is rising up inside of me. It could be triggered by words to a song, something I see on TV, a scene in a movie, a sad article or story I have just read, a memory that suddenly comes to my mind, a reflection of something or sometimes absolutely nothing at all. As I feel the wave about to hit me, I find a place to sit down, (often on the floor) and I just let my emotions out. It usually lasts a few minutes and then it goes away.

I used to dread these moments and would resist and fight them off with everything I had when I felt them coming on. But if I was successful, they would usually hit me a few hours later twice as hard, and so I slowly learned to just embrace them when they were happening. And it's ok. When they are over I usually pray and thank God for allowing me to get through it and for hearing any questions or venting as I'm grieving. And you know what? I'm not embarrassed about it. It's ok because I know with certainty that it's a part of a healthy grieving process and has helped me to heal in the long run. And as time has gone by, there are less and less waves of grief to ride out and they are shorter in duration.

You need to remember that you also went through cycles during your abusive relationship that came with their own set of emotional ups and downs. It shouldn't be too surprising that the memories of these moments might evoke the same range of emotions. Because of your resilience, you were able to ride a seemingly endless roller coaster of emotions, before you took the courageous step of leaving your abuser.

Have you ever noticed that when you climb off a roller coaster you often still feel some of the motions from the ride for a few minutes after? Now apply that to the relationship you have been through and realize that it lasted months or years, not just a few minutes. Do you see how normal the cycles of grief can be now?

Perhaps what will be the most baffling to you is the fact that you know from the deepest depths of your heart that you had to get out. You know without a doubt that leaving was a better alternative than staying. You know it was ultimately your choice and your decision to leave your abuser (unless you were with a narcissist who left you). Yet you still have these intense feelings of grief that can be all-consuming. You can't understand why you have moments when you feel a strong desire to return, despite knowing that the relationship was bad, and that your abuser was really hurtful to you. You might find yourself questioning or doubting your decision to leave and wonder, why?

What is happening is that you are subconsciously still maintaining the cycles from your abusive relationship. The ups and downs, the emotional highs and lows, the back and forth, and everything in between. It's that roller coaster, only now your mind is also remembering your thoughts, decisions and responses to the cycles of abuse you were experiencing. Think about the pattern that played itself out, over and over again.

Each incident of lying, condemning, yelling, screaming, cursing, belittling and shunning is usually followed by periods of kindness, acknowledgment and remorse (if you're lucky) and affection. Or there is at least a "down" period where your abuser isn't acting up or out as much. These moments of "softness" can be comforting and bring you hope. They can create a sense of false security and reassurance (albeit brief) again. You gain renewed hope and you want to believe your abuser has turned a corner. Unfortunately, this allows your abuser to pull you back in again, and the cycle of abuse repeats. These conflicting emotions that you are feeling can create a confusing but very intense and even addictive attachment. And so, as you go through the process of grieving, you will wrestle with the memories of these same moments again and again.

There is another aspect of these cycles that many survivors don't realize. There are the obvious conflicting parts of your abusive partner; they can be loving, caring, comforting and affectionate one minute and mean, abusive and distant the next. Now throw in the fact that your abuser uses their supposed "good" qualities to confuse, manipulate and control you. Their kindness is not actually real, it is a weapon from their toolbox to control you, hurt you and take advantage of you. Think about how sick a person has to be in order to act like that. Think about the emotional confusion that can create inside of you when you are able to grasp the reality of this. And when you do, use it as a reminder of why you should never, ever return to that psychotic human being.

Earlier in this book I talked about losing and regaining your identity as a result of the abuse you endured. It is important to remember that you are, or likely will also grieve the loss of your identity or "self" that took place during the relationship. Your abuser probably dismissed and negated most of your feelings, needs or ideas, and as a result you learned to dismiss and deny those very things so vital to one's personal identity. We are often either shamed out of our feelings, likes, dislikes, values and opinions, or we hide them so that we can survive the abuse.

Our grief over our loss of identity is often enhanced by the damage the abuse did to our confidence and our self-esteem. We convince ourselves that we "allowed" this to happen instead of recognizing that this was a basic human "response" to the abuse. We blame ourselves for "choosing" to distance ourselves from our children, friends and family to satisfy our abuser's needs, insecurities, jealousy, possessiveness and desire to isolate us. And yes, we have to ultimately own those decisions, but we can't lose sight of the fact that our actions were in response to our abuser's demands, manipulation and control. And so, we often also grieve our sense of blame, guilt, shame and the loneliness that comes from that withdrawal, isolation and loss of self.

Perhaps the thing we might grieve the most is that our abuser turned out to be someone we couldn't possibly imagine at the beginning of the relationship. In fact, because denial plays such a strong role in helping us cope with the abuse we receive, there's a strong likelihood that you won't truly grasp how toxic the person is until the relationship is over. And hindsight can be painful. Once you have a chance to look back, away from and outside of the relationship, you will be better able to see all the red flags you missed, the soft and subtle ways you were seduced, manipulated and controlled, and all of the times you ignored it or flat out missed it.

The simple fact is that the person you fell in love with and poured your heart into wasn't who they claimed to be. You may grieve that they didn't try to address their toxic behavior. That they didn't try to build up the relationship but instead chose to tear it down. You may grieve that the love of your life, didn't feel the same way about you. You may grieve over the fact that they actually faked many of the feelings you thought were genuine. Yet you still may miss them.

That's because they were an important part of your life for a while. You loved and cared for them, and there were good times in the midst of all the bad ones. And you will miss *those* times. And it's ok. Don't feel bad about the good moments you enjoyed with this person. They happened, they were real to you, and they mattered. It's ok to grieve and even look back at those moments with fondness and miss them. Don't pass judgment on *your* genuine feelings. Have compassion on yourself.

Remember that your emotional abuser doesn't feel the same way you do. They can't really feel at all. How sad. Emotional abusers are unhealthy individuals, most of which are not capable of feeling and displaying normal human emotions. The world they live in is devoid of the very sensitivities that most of us take for granted in our lives on a daily basis. Imagine not having the ability to truly feel love, joy, grace, tenderness, jubilation or empathy and sympathy for others.

Imagine only having the ability to fake those behaviors by mimicking those who actually can feel it. Imagine the anger and jealousy you might feel knowing there is something lacking in your life but either not knowing why, or seeing it lived out in others and not having the ability to experience what most people get to feel. That is the world of an abuser who suffers from Cluster B disorders. Over time, hopefully you can grieve over them in a different way, from that perspective.

There is one other aspect that many survivors of abuse grieve over that is often dismissed because it is perceived as non-emotional, and therefore not worth grieving, and that is the financial challenges (and often loss) that you can experience from a divorce or the end of a deep, committed relationship. In many cases the abuser doesn't come into the relationship with a lot of assets of their own, and they are often in the relationship mainly to take some or all of what is yours.

Not only did they probably strain or drain your finances during the relationship because of their demands, high needs and insatiable appetite to acquire things, but they will also make every effort to take what they feel they deserve at the end of it. And when you add just the basic logistical and financial challenges of moving, paying final bills, closing accounts, opening new ones and getting re-established somewhere new, you can see how "finances" can further challenge you in the grieving process.

For some survivors, there is also the subconscious grieving that takes place over not going into familiar places (if you move) that you used to frequent, and having to re-orient yourself to your new surroundings. This can also be complicated by the feeling of not wanting to go to certain places for fear or concern of running into your abuser, because you don't know how you would react if you see them, let alone have to talk to them.

You may become wary of the emotions that might be triggered from that type of encounter. You might feel like you just can't escape the person or you want to do everything you can to avoid them. But that's the old abuse talking. You just have to remind yourself that you don't owe that person anything. Zip, nada, nothing. Sure, don't be careless and put yourself in a potentially uncomfortable situation, but don't be afraid to live your life either. Let them worry about themselves. You have enough to deal with and grieve for.

It is important to keep in mind that your emotions are your internal compass, and healthy grieving is a part of those emotions. It is basically your body's way of telling you to pay attention because something has happened to you. And toxic relationships have a way of evoking strong emotions. Just remember that sometimes the feelings that you are feeling on the surface may be masking the core emotion that is stirring deeper inside of you. You may be feeling angry on the outside, but beneath that feeling is the guilt and shame you have internalized over staying in the relationship so long.

It is important to process and validate all of your feelings. They are your exclusive feelings, and you are entitled to have them and not feel guilty about them. Have compassion on yourself and the losses you have suffered. Take your time and re-connect with your hopes, dreams and values, and then search for and rediscover your purpose to help rebuild your self-esteem.

Make time to re-engage in life and fill your life with friends, family and other important things. Take the time to try something new or other things that bring you joy. Visit some place new, or an old favorite that is connected with good times and memories. Don't let grieving be your only activity. And please realize that you are not alone.

Whether you believe in Him or not, God is grieving right there with you. When you hurt, He hurts, and He wants to help you find your joy again. The Bible tells us in Psalm 34:18 that

> *"The Lord is close to the brokenhearted and saves those who are crushed in spirit."*

Our relationships were meant to be healthy, whole and nourishing. They were not meant for dissension, sorrow and abuse. God knows that you are hurting from the brokenness of your relationship. He is the Healer not just of your body but also your spirit and emotions.

Reach out to Jesus and ask Him to heal and comfort you. He is after all,

> *"The Father of compassion and the God of all comfort, who comforts us in all our troubles."* 2 Corinthians 1:4

You don't need to suppress your grief, nor does it need to bury you. God isn't immune to grief and He's certainly not indifferent to it. He has experienced it at the deepest level possible when His Son died on the cross for you and me. And this same God is with us in our grief. He doesn't always tell us why we're suffering, but he does offer us himself. Matthew 5:4 says:

"Blessed are those who mourn, for they will be comforted."

At the heart of the Christian faith is a Father in Heaven who says He's always with us—and who has faced grief and loss the same way we have. Isaiah 53:3 describes Jesus as "*a man of sorrows and familiar with suffering.*" John 11:34 tells us that when Jesus experienced the death of his close friend Lazarus, "*he wept.*" This is a Father who feels what we feel, grieves when we grieve and can completely relate to what you are going through. Cry out to Him and He surely will comfort you as only a loving Father can.

9

Understanding and Dealing with Anger

After being in an emotionally abusive relationship with someone who suffers from Cluster B disorders, survivors are often caught in a confusing set of emotions that include frustration, regret, sadness, hopelessness and often perpetual anger. While you are working through the emotions of healing from abuse and trauma, many abuse survivors are caught off guard by the fact that they experience quite a bit of anger, and sometimes even rage, which can often linger for quite some time after they leave the relationship.

This makes sense for obvious reasons, but the underlying factor is the sudden awareness that our situation is fundamentally unfair. To make matters worse, there's no reasonable justification for what has happened to us, since it wasn't because of something we did. We may fluctuate between being angry at our abuser for all of the pain and confusion they have caused us, and we may also be angry at ourselves for either allowing ourselves to get into the relationship in the first place, or allowing and tolerating our Cluster B to abuse, control, manipulate and take advantage of us for so long.

The main difference between whether people end up feeling hopeless or angry seems to come down to whether they end up blaming themselves or their abusers for what is happening. Being able to feel angry about being abused is, in general, a good thing. Anger has the capability of acting as a motivating force. Anger's ability to motivate is never stronger than in situations in which people feel they have been put down unjustly and that they have a right to take action to correct their situation. This is often referred to as a righteous anger and can be a healthy emotion.

In order to deal with the traumatic effects of emotional abuse and ultimately heal from them, we have to be able to bring everything that has happened to us and what we feel, to the forefront. We have to expose it, lay it all out so-to-speak, look at it, process it, and then deal with it. This is because while we are still in the middle of the abuse, we normally don't bring it forward; we just find ways to endure it by suppressing our emotions. In fact, we often mentally disconnect from our painful experiences as they are happening. We feel the pain but we aren't really processing and connecting it with anything.

Even when there are moments when we fight back, argue or defend ourselves with our abuser, we often deny the emotional and physical pain we are feeling at the time in order to stay in the relationship. I know this sounds a little crazy, but if we didn't employ this defense mechanism, our feelings would overwhelm us. Eventually they do, which is what finally forces us to leave, or helps us decide to leave our abuser. More often than not, the main emotion we feel during an abusive episode is hurt and sadness, not anger.

Because of our subconscious need to disassociate in order to survive our abusive situation, many survivors often have a delayed reaction to being victimized. We aren't able to get the clarity we need to grasp the impact of the violation until we get away from our abuser. Once we aren't in the abusive environment on a daily basis anymore, the anger we suppressed and internalized during the abuse comes out. And because it has been suppressed for so long, it often comes out in the form of severe anger and rage.

Anger is one of those emotions that can be difficult for many people to process and deal with, especially survivors of emotional abuse. It can be difficult to know what to do with it and where to direct it. What makes it even harder to deal with is the fact that the person we want to focus all of our anger, rage and frustration on is not available to us to receive it. And so, we have this completely natural human survival response that is there to protect us from threat and harm, and we now have nowhere and no one to let it out on. We are in essence robbed of the satisfaction of releasing the anger we feel on the source of that anger.

The good thing is that the anger you are feeling will help you go from feeling like a helpless victim, to a hardy, indignant survivor. Leaving your abuser is an amazing achievement of personal independence, and that's a very empowering step in the right direction. You are no longer someone else's verbal punching bag.

You are rediscovering that you are a special and independent person who deserves to be treated with respect and dignity by others. And this is all part of our evolution of understanding what it is like to go from being a victim, to becoming a survivor. The anger you feel from becoming an undeserved victim has become the fuel and motivation you need to find the strength to heal from the pain you felt during your relationship.

Letting Your Anger Go

Once you are away from your abuser, it is imperative to let out any anger you are feeling completely. Your emotions and every part of your body need to fully register the feelings of the offenses that were committed against you to protect you against someone who might cross your boundaries, or is potentially abusive or controlling in the future. There's plenty of constructive ways to let your anger out including exercise, crying out, screaming, writing out the anger you feel

HEALING FROM A TOXIC AND ABUSIVE RELATIONSHIP

or incorporating releasing techniques you can learn from a good counselor or therapist.

In a perfect world, our anger not only motivates us to leave our abusive situations, but it also helps us to vent and let out all of the pain
and suppressed emotions we felt during the relationship. Fully feeling
the impact of what happened to us actually helps us to eventually learn
more about ourselves, our abuser and the nature of human beings. It
is one of the many aspects in our healing journey that allows us to
move forward and get beyond our previous self-identification as a victim. Our anger can come in cycles or pop up unexpectedly as certain
buried memories come to the forefront and we grieve and wrestle
with them.

But you need to realize that it is not good to live your life angry all of
the time. In fact, prolonged anger is literally bad for your health. (That's
one of the issues our abusers have). Normally, our anger resolves itself
as the memories and pain we feel are processed and dealt with. But,
for some people, the anger just continues in a never-ending cycle of
emotion.

The longer that anger hangs around, the less useful it becomes, until it
starts to hinder your recovery. It can actually turn into a mental, physical and social health problem and can rob you of your happiness. At
that point, if you haven't started working with an abuse counselor yet,
it is imperative that you do so, to help you address and free yourself
from the anger you still feel.

Memories of abuse tend not to fade away too easily. You may still feel
embarrassed, manipulated and taken advantage of. And it may still hurt.
And the longer you endured your abusive situation the longer you will
feel all of the negative emotions that come from it, including anger.

The emotional impact of abuse memories may or may not fade with
time, but no amount of time will ever completely erase the knowledge

that the abuse occurred. Our memories tend to be a one-way street. But if you remain backwards-looking for too long, and just continue to rehash them over and over, you may never get any closure and you may never be able to move forward.

While it is completely understandable if this occurs, it's still not healthy. People who remain angry and bitter and spend most of their time thinking about past offenses and injustices tend not to be very happy (think your abuser). When you remain angry for too long you will in essence start to oppress yourself which allows your abuser to continue to hurt you even though they no longer are in your life.

While we may often believe that the main source of our anger is our abuser, there are going to be moments when we may realize that we are also angry at ourselves. Sometimes it's helpful to understand who your anger is directed at so that you can direct your processing and healing responses in the right direction toward properly addressing the correct source of your anger.

Grab two pieces of paper, and at the top of one write "Abuser" and at the top of the other write "Myself." Each time you are feeling angry, ask yourself "Am I really angry at my abuser or at myself?" Then ask yourself, "Why am I angry at this person? What did he or she do? How does this make me feel? Write down your answers or findings on the appropriate sheet and then work through them with a skilled counselor.

It can be fairly easy to pinpoint the memory of the action(s) that makes us feel angry. You might have been verbally or physically attacked, criticized, insulted, forced or manipulated to do something you didn't want to do--ignored, treated unfairly or blamed for something you didn't do. But we can only make progress on addressing and healing from those actions when we can truly understand how those actions actually make us feel.

Did or does it make you feel annoyed, anxious, deceived, disrespected, frustrated, guilty, helpless, humiliated, invalidated, powerless, rejected, resentful or sad? All of those can be feelings associated with your anger. And it's *those* feelings you need to work through as much as the action that caused you to feel those emotions in the first place.

You may have to make a new list a few times to work through each offense or emotion as they emerge in your memory. But once you work through them, I encourage you to give them up and release them to God. And then throw the list in the garbage. You can even make a ceremony of this each time you work through a list. Just go outside and light that list on fire and watch it disappear.

It's imperative that you do this because it serves no constructive purpose to keep your list of offenses after you have addressed them. The whole goal of the exercise is to work through your feelings, and release the anger and bitterness attached to each offense so you can move on from them and return to a place of love. Because the Bible tells us in 1 Corinthians 13:5 that one of the attributes of love is that *"It keeps no record of wrongs."*

The way anger feels varies from person to person. All of us have different ways of processing and responding to anger, especially if we are feeling emotions we haven't felt before. The more we understand how we feel about a problem or offense, the better able we are to deal with it. Most people probably think they are only angry about the situation, person or incident, but there are usually more personalized and internal emotions boiling beneath that anger.

In fact, what we think caused our anger might actually have triggered something in us that is entirely separate from the things that we actually believe caused the anger. This is often referred to as underlying anger. More often than not, it comes from something we either fear or from a previous wound or relevant hurt we have experienced before. And *that* is actually the root cause of the anger we are feeling at that moment.

Anger is an integral part of our body's "fight, flight, or freeze" system, which helps protect us from threats or danger. This defense mechanism allows us to survive, adapt, and defend, making it a necessary survival instinct. It is an emotion which has the primary intention of solving whatever problem or situation that we are facing. It can give us the energy and the strength to both motivate us and to allow us to face that problem in the hopes of resolving it. This is the purpose and general feeling of anger, and it is a completely normal and natural feeling to have. But there comes a point when we need to let that anger go. And that's not always easy since memories of our abuse tend to stick with us for a long time.

The anger we initially felt that gave us the strength to leave our abuser, and help direct and process the pain we felt from the abusive relationship eventually should no longer be needed. Thus it is worthwhile to work hard, reduce its intensity and frequency, and let it go. This is not always an easy transition to make, but it is an extremely necessary one. That's because feeling and staying angry for long periods of time has negative consequences on both your physical and emotional well-being.

Prolonged anger can make you feel tired, drained, sick and unable to focus. It can affect your appetite, give you high blood pressure and make you even more angry. And then you become a person no one wants to be around. So let it out, process it, understand it, deal with it and then let it go. Remind yourself that the best "revenge" you could possibly have on your abuser is to live well and be happy. Life is just too short to live any other way.

10

Stabilizing after Abuse

Once you have left your abuser and the non-stop emotional abuse is finally over, you tend to expect that you are going to start feeling good again. You might feel reasonably sure your abuser isn't going to harass you anymore, and you have taken all of the normal, practical steps you need to take to live in a new home and start a new life again. And yet, as I mentioned earlier, you still grieve, have plenty of moments of anger, pain and a deep sense of loss. Your confidence and self-esteem may be shattered, and you wonder where the old you has gone and what is going to become of the current you. Even though you chose to leave, that deep sense of loss you are feeling is probably going to stick around for a while. That's because healing from emotional abuse takes time.

Change can be unsettling for anybody. But because you've experienced trauma from emotional abuse, you may feel especially stressed when you experience all of the new changes you have been forced to make in your life. That's because abuse of any kind strips us of the ability to feel safe in the world. You have just been shown and experienced the darkest sides of someone who suffers from Cluster B disorders. It was your spouse/partner and lover – someone you trusted and hoped to live with for the rest of your days. Someone you made a life-long commitment to. Someone with whom you trusted and shared your innermost being. And you were betrayed in the deepest sense of the word.

And now you wonder if you can ever feel safe with anyone again. Even though it's quiet and you no longer face your abuser's continuous barrage of toxic behavior, you find the quiet unsettling. You may now be constantly on edge, and you may have a heightened awareness for anything that might possibly go wrong in your life. You start to doubt everyone and question everything. And you hate this. Memories of the abuse, constantly flood your mind and fill your thoughts. You feel them over and over again and just to add injury to insult, you make new discoveries of manipulation, lies and deception that you either weren't aware of before, or that your mind instinctively shut out at the time it happened. *This* is the toughest part of surviving abuse. This is part of the trauma.

You didn't want to make this life change; you were forced into it. And it's quite normal to have negative thoughts and feelings about the change you are experiencing. In fact, it can be much more difficult for a survivor of emotional abuse to feel comfortable with a new place or situation because your body interprets the change as *danger*.

This is because trauma alters the way our brain, emotional energy and nervous system respond to an event or action. If our mind and body can't process what happened to make us feel safe afterward, it re-activates sooner or to slighter perceptions of change going forward. We basically have a heightened sense of awareness to any type of potential danger. This is what's often referred to as *hyperarousal*.

At the other end of the emotional spectrum is *hypoarousal*. This happens when a survivor of abuse becomes so affected and overwhelmed by the trauma they have experienced that their body and mind just start to shut down. A person who is responding like this often acts depressed or burned out and doesn't seem to care about anything anymore. It takes every effort to get up out of bed and face the day ahead of you. You may often feel like you are in a perpetual state of numbness to everything and everyone around you. You just can't seem to feel anything.

What is happening is that your nervous system is attempting to work as nature intended it to, in order to protect you and keep you safe by avoiding risk and danger. Unfortunately, your body is responding negatively and excessively to the impact of the trauma you experienced, which results in having a lower tolerance for any type of emotional activity. Because you've spent so many months or years protecting your emotions, you may have cut yourself off from them. Even though you know you have reason to feel happy and liberated, you just can't muster up any emotion. And this can cause you to miss out on rebuilding relationships, getting involved in new activities or even enjoying the simple pleasures in life. It becomes a struggle just to get through the day without giving in to the overwhelming number of negative emotions you feel.

Addressing your conscious and subconscious fears can build new strengths that enable you to experience a more positive and fulfilling post-traumatic life. I like to call this distress tolerance, and it might be one of the most important skills you ever learn. It's not about pretending your world is a safer place because you are no longer with your abuser. It basically entails becoming comfortable with your discomfort. It requires that you identify and validate the discomfort you have and are feeling, and then start to feel safe with those anxieties, fears and worries you have.

Once you have identified what they are, and validated that it's ok to feel them, you need to share them with someone you trust, preferably a professional counselor, therapist or support group who can help you work through them. It's important to understand that there's nothing wrong with having these fears and concerns. The key is to not let them dominate and control your life. Otherwise, your abuser wins and is still able to have a negative effect on you. It takes time to feel safe and comfortable again, but it will happen.

There are a few things you can do on your own that will also help you build up your tolerance to change and help you manage your emotional energy levels. Take a few moments every day to notice the things that are still the same in your life even after your big change has occurred, and focus on them. It could be objects or possessions that you still have, routines, places you like to go to, your job, certain friends, family members or even pets that are still in your life. Focus on your senses - what you see and hear, and the people and things around you. For me, going for a walk or a hike enables me to experience that. Listen to a lot of music and really pay attention to the lyrics of songs you like.

Finally, recognize and remind yourself that you are a survivor. You have proven that you have the strength and wisdom to make wise decisions and the changes necessary to make your life better. You have the ability to deal with what makes you anxious and stressed and you *can* keep yourself safe. You no longer are tolerating abuse or experiencing the trauma of your past. You still have an amazing future ahead of you. Embrace it.

Rebuilding

It can be easy to lose yourself while you are in an abusive relationship. When it's over, you may question who you are without that person who was constantly traumatizing you. You finally found the courage to say, "Enough is enough" and say goodbye to this person you once loved and gave your heart to. But you may also feel like damaged goods, especially if your abuser consistently put you down and criticized you all the time.

Your self-esteem and your sense of identity have been shattered by the person who was supposed to love and cherish you. And often complicating things can be the fact that maybe you still love your abuser despite everything they did to you. Maybe your heart aches from missing him or her, and remembering the good times you had together. Sometimes the good memories suddenly monopolize your thoughts and you start to feel guilty for leaving them.

Regardless of what finally triggered you to leave your abuser, you somehow knew on a rational level that your abuser was not a healthy functioning human being and you needed to leave the relationship. There are probably so many emotions, thoughts, and memories swirling around in your head that you question what is real, what is true, and what is right for you.

And this is what can make being finally free from the abuse feel so disorienting. Yes, you no longer are experiencing the constant torture of your abuser and your life is your own now. You are now free to live your life without being in a constant state of fear and stress. Free to make decisions that fulfill your needs and put yourself first. But there's another part of you that feels devastated, and you spend a lot of time wondering what you should do and where to go from here. And it can take time to find yourself again.

Leaving and ending an emotionally abusive relationship is almost like experiencing a death. I can tell you this first-hand because I lost my first wife to cancer after more than thirty years together, and I left the abusive relationship that followed after close to four years. And in both cases, you simply cannot rush the grieving, anger and healing process. You simply must go through the stages of grief and anger to get to the stages of emotional healing. You have to constantly remind yourself that you were placed in this position because of your abuser and that eventually you will heal and move on from this unfortunate season in your life.

Just as with anger, I strongly recommend that you write down and journal your feelings of grief and disappointment, but also the hopes and dreams you might have for the future. Think about the things you couldn't do with your abuser, that you might be able to do now. What are some new things you want to learn and do, or places you want to visit or trips you might want to take in the future. You may not be able to do them all right away, but they will give you something positive to look forward to.

Another thing that has probably taken a huge hit from your abusive relationship is your self-esteem. You may not like yourself very much right now. You may be tempted to blame yourself for allowing the abuse or worse yet, triggering it in your abuser. Don't. You are an amazing and worthy person. You can slowly rebuild your self-esteem by accomplishing small goals, like cleaning your home, getting rid of things you no longer need or things that can remind you of your abuser. Perhaps take a night class, pick up a hobby, join a gym, learn how to dance and join a dance community, volunteer somewhere, join a church if you don't belong to one, or volunteer on a missions trip. At this point, almost anything you do will give you a small sense of satisfaction and hope.

Once you have settled into your new surroundings and developed a new routine, try to set aside some time to re-examine your values, opinions and beliefs. You will often find that some of the things that were important to you before the relationship, no longer are. And as a result of the trauma there may be new things that mean more to you now. Look at any area of your life in which your abuser controlled the decisions, and come up with your own point of view or preferences. This is an opportunity to create the new you. Wrap your arms around the process and embrace it.

Don't Revisit the Past

Lastly, listen to the voice inside your head, not the feelings that are coming from your heart. I can tell you without a doubt, that it is easy to love someone even though you know they are not only a bad person but also bad for you. You probably will experience those moments of doubt when your heart tells you to consider giving your abuser one more chance. It might remind you of the good times you had together, especially at the beginning of the relationship. There may be nights you feel really lonely and you will hurt so bad you can barely stand it.

You might want to look at your old photos or look up your abuser on social media to see how they are doing. Resist the temptation and instead call a friend or family member who can remind you of all the right reasons that made you leave the relationship. Deep down inside you know you made the right decision to leave your abuser. You can see and feel how much damage they have done to you. Out there in that great big world, there's someone that will be perfect for you, someone who truly knows how to love you and will appreciate all of the unique and wonderful things about you. If you were to go back to your abuser you'll never get the chance to meet them and have another opportunity for genuine love and affection.

And speaking of that potential new love that may be out there waiting for that divine appointment with you, give yourself some time before you go searching for it. You need to love, heal and care for yourself first before you even think about a new relationship. You have much to learn about yourself, and recovery takes time. Give yourself some space to grow. Don't just try to plug in somebody new to fill that empty void you have. Most people who do, eventually live to regret it, and the last thing you need right now is to deal with more potential relational fallout.

Jumping into another relationship right away won't help you heal. You'll just bring all your wounds and brokenness into the next relationship and create a big mess. Trying to find your worth from another relationship right away or from anywhere or anything else won't help you find the healing you desire. After you've left an abusive marriage, it's your golden opportunity to find your self-worth from the right places, by respecting yourself and by accepting that you're truly loved by Jesus.

Things Left Unsaid

There is one more thing I want to address that is very important not to overlook in the healing process and that is dealing with things that were left unsaid. Now you may have had a final big blowup in which you were able to vent and release everything you had been feeling about your abuser, but normally those opportunities are rare. Often you leave the situation fairly quickly and don't have the time, or you're too hurt and weak to share what is really on your mind, you can't even properly extrapolate what you feel, or your abuser doesn't give you an opportunity to properly do so.

And now that you have left them and are starting to feel stronger again, it's too late to go back and tell them how badly they hurt you. Now that you are finally able, you have no way to stand up for yourself and represent how you truly feel. Stick with the no contact rule, and instead write a letter to your abuser. Just don't send it to them. I hate to say this, but I can promise you they probably could care less how you feel anyway.

But it is important that you articulate everything that is going through your mind. Include all of the memories, moments and pain. Writing helps you to slow down your thoughts and start to become more aware of your emotions. You can even write it in the form of a letter, poem or song. Whatever works best for you, just get it all out and then let it go. I can assure you that over time, the emotions you are feeling will fade away.

11

Healing from Emotional Abuse

An abuser makes their partner's/spouse's world small by design. The smaller your world is, the bigger their place is in it, until they're all your world is. When this happens, you have very little choice but to tiptoe around them, follow all of their demands and work around every whim and mood fluctuation they have throughout the day. The cruel irony is that part of the reason you feel so terrible when you no longer have an abuser in your life, is that there is a huge gap where 90% of your energy and attention used to be focused.

The good news is that you now have an opportunity to fill that gap with things that benefit you and help you to heal. There comes a point when you will have fully recognized the impact of the victimization you have experienced, processed it, and can begin to believe that the trauma you experienced is no longer going to be the defining principle in your life.

It is time to redefine yourself and show the world (and yourself) that you are stronger than what happened to you. You need to absolutely own your recovery and take charge of your recovery process. Ultimately, this is something only *you* can change. And there are definitely some ways to make that happen sooner rather than later.

First of all, as I have mentioned before, take care of the basics. A healthy body feeds a healthy mind and vice versa. Make sure you get enough sleep and adequate rest. The abusive trauma you experienced will often mess with your sleep patterns so it is important to pay attention to that. Eat a healthy diet that includes lots of fruits and vegetables. Drink plenty of water. If you don't currently exercise on a regular basis, start. It will help you release any anger you are feeling and it's just plain good for you. Go for plenty of walks or do some hiking.

Don't Try Finding Quick Cures

It won't help to try to endlessly numb yourself with alcohol, drugs or other addictions. It won't make you feel any better and just slows down your recovery. And even if you don't do those things, there are other ways we often employ to fool ourselves into trying to help numb the pain. It's easy to just stay busy, immersing ourselves in projects, endlessly volunteering or helping others, going shopping, watching TV or listening to music all day to numb ourselves and avoid having to deal with our emotions, pain and memories.

Sometimes seeking relief from the pain and sadness you are feeling at a particular moment can seem like the prudent thing to do or your only option, especially when you are feeling confused about how to move forward. But sooner or later, what you avoid dealing with in the present will come back to hurt you later. And in the process you may miss out on what God truly wants for you, (which is always better than what we can possibly imagine).

Working with a Therapist

The single most important thing you can do is talk to someone who understands your situation. Emotional abuse is not as widely understood as other forms of abuse. People who don't have experience or knowledge about this form of abuse will have difficulty empathizing and offering support and sound advice. Talking with friends can be helpful to vent, but unless they have experienced emotional abuse firsthand, they will not understand emotional abuse like a professional counselor or licensed therapist would, and they will often fall into habits of victim-blaming or telling you how to think and what to do.

If and when you do seek the help of a counselor, it's important to make sure to find a therapist or counselor that is familiar with or special-izes in emotional abuse. While a biblically based, family, marriage or lay counselor may often be found for free at your local church, or a general counselor might be less expensive, they most likely won't have the tools or skills to help you.

In fact, abuse victims often expose themselves to becoming revictim-ized at churches or with inexperienced counselors who lack training or because of outdated or biblically incorrect thinking. And yes, this is coming from a Christian believer. You'll know if you are talking to the wrong person if you hear statements like, "You need to honor your marriage no matter what" or "you enabled the abuse" or idiotic questions like "What was your role in the abuse or relationship prob-lems?" or "What did you do to cause your abuser to get so angry? etc." Remember, you did nothing to cause or justify the abuse and you had no part in it!

Abuse survivors who spend years in basic counseling for abuse and don't get better often blame themselves for not making very little, if any, progress in their recovery. But the problem isn't with them; it's because they are seeing a counselor who isn't really familiar with the trauma and effects of abuse or hasn't been trained in it. You owe it to yourself to see a specialist, not a general practitioner.

A skilled counselor is trained to help people who have suffered abuse. They will be able to talk with you about your specific circumstances, and then educate and help you to understand that being abused is never acceptable and is certainly never your fault. To get help, you need to first acknowledge that there is a problem. You can't change anything until you acknowledge there's a problem in the first place.

A good counselor can also offer you a safe place to process what you are going through. This is especially important if you're suffering from anxiety, depression or PTSD. And if you cannot afford to go to a counselor, there are some counselors who have sliding scales which make it more affordable. You can also check out churches which sometimes offer lay counselors for free. Even the Bible promotes counseling (Proverbs 11:14, and 15:22).

Society often looks down on counseling and gives it a negative stereotype. They look at it as a sign of weakness and vulnerability. But it is actually a sign of courage, humility, strength and wisdom to seek advice from someone who knows more about a subject than you do and can help guide you to feel better about yourself and your future. Why would anyone not want that outcome? You may not feel courageous in seeking professional help, but you are. Your bravery, determination and perseverance will see you through this dark period in your life, and you will come out shining on the other end. Just give it time.

Consider joining an abuse recovery support group. Aside from therapy, it can be incredibly reaffirming to speak to people who have had a similar experience to what you have gone through. Listening to other people's similar experiences will help you realize with complete clarity that what happened to you was not because you did something wrong, but rather it was from a very deliberate campaign by your abuser.

Hearing how other people have felt like they lost their identity and direction in life can also help ease the feeling of being alone in what you are going through. After all, making you feel alone was the end goal your abuser always wanted to achieve in order to exert more control over you. Some people think of support groups as a misery-loves-company idea, but it is exactly the opposite. It can be tremendously empowering.

At some point in your recovery process, you eventually need to make peace with what happened to you and make peace with your abuser (more on that later). There comes a point where you need to be able to accept what happened to you and no longer ruminate over it. One of the most empowering things that my counselor helped me with was dealing with the fact that my abuser didn't and couldn't share the same feelings and emotions of love toward me as I had for her, and that the whole relationship had been an act of manipulation to get what she wanted from me.

One day he asked me this simple question: "Greyson, was what you felt toward her real to you?" I agreed. He then asked me, "Can you be ok with that? What if that's all you get from the relationship? That *you* felt something for this person, and that what she said and did actually *felt* real to you and it mattered, even if it wasn't." And that has become my new personal survivor's mantra - *It was real, it happened and it mattered.* To me. And I'm ok with that now.

A number of recent studies on emotional abuse found that when we experience rejection of any kind like emotional abuse, we actually activate the same regions in the brain as we do when we experience physical pain. When emotional abuse is allowed to continue, it has the ability to damage our deepest core. We start to internalize and believe the hurtful things that a person says. This is why it is so important not to allow the abuse to continue in our head long after we have left our abusive relationship. Continuing to reinforce the pain you felt when you were being abused through constant negative and ruminating thoughts months or years later will only prevent you from healing and moving on in your life.

Lean Into God

One of the things that really helped me in my personal recovery was leaning into God, praying to Him and asking for His guidance. Anytime I would feel anxious or sad I would remind myself of God's love for me, His character and kindness. Philippians 4:6-7 says

"Do not be anxious about anything, but in every situation, by prayer and petition, with thanksgiving, present your requests to God. And the peace of God, which transcends all understanding, will guard your hearts and your minds in Christ Jesus."

God encourages us to pray when we are feeling anxious about anything. Then God promises to give us peace. And He can be trusted.

God is sovereign and even when things feel out of control for me, I know He is still in control. No matter how stressed I feel, or how worried about something I may be, I know that God is bigger and stronger than my problem(s). Proverbs 3:5-6 says:

"Trust in the Lord with all your heart and lean not on your own understanding; in all your ways acknowledge him, and He will make your paths straight."

We humans are finite beings, so our minds are limited. But God is infinite. There are no boundaries for Him because he is the Author and Creator of all things. When we need to lean on Him, God promises that he will direct our path and show us what to do.

God also tells us that we do not have to be afraid. Not of our abuser, our present situation, or the future. In fact, the phrase "Fear Not" is the most commonly mentioned phrase in the Bible. No matter what makes us afraid or concerned, God is bigger and stronger. Psalm 56:3-4 says

"When I am afraid, I will trust in you. In God, whose word I praise, In God I trust; I will not be afraid. What can mortal man do to me?"

No matter what fear, threat or trouble you are facing, God can take care of you and help you overcome it.

I also really want to encourage you to not just talk to God but to also read His Word in the Bible. Learning what God has to say can really help you reject the lies you heard about yourself from your abuser and give you a new sense of identity instead of feeling like a failure. When you learn who you are in Christ, you can unlearn the things you were told about yourself by your abuser and learn that you are beautifully made and truly loved and accepted just as you are by Jesus.

You are a child of God. John 1:12-13

> "Yet to all who did receive him, to those who believed in his name, he gave the right to become children of God— children born not of natural descent, nor of human decision or a husband's will, but born of God."

God loves you unconditionally. I John 4:16

> "So we have come to know and to believe the love that God has for us. God is love, and whoever abides in love abides in God, and God abides in him."

Your sense of identity lies with God, not your abuser. You are a survivor, not a victim or a failure. If you do not know Jesus personally I want to encourage you to ask Him into your heart and into your life. God's Word in I John 4:14 says

> "If **anyone** acknowledges that Jesus is the Son of God, God lives in him and he in us. And so we know and rely on the love God has for us."

Don't try and travel down this road of recovery on your own, let God guide you and comfort you. I want to encourage you to pray a Prayer of Salvation. Please realize that it's not the prayer that saves; it's the repentance and faith behind the prayer that lays hold of salvation. But you can pray something like this:

Heavenly Father, thank you for creating me and loving me. I know that I am a sinner and that I cannot save myself. By faith I gratefully receive your Salvation. I am ready to trust you as my Lord and Savior. Jesus, I believe you are Son of God, who came to earth, died on the cross for my sins, and rose from the dead on the third day. Thank you for bearing my sins and giving me the gift of eternal life. I believe your words are true. Come into my heart and be my Lord and Savior. I pray this in Jesus' name, Amen

Give God Your Guilt and Shame

Because of who Jesus is, and our decision to accept his sacrifice, we have a new identity. No longer do we have to see ourselves as victims. We can begin to see ourselves as victors. God tells us in Romans 8:1 that:

"There is no condemnation for those of us who have accepted Jesus as our Lord and Savior."

So, the next time you feel guilty about leaving your abuser, remember that Jesus took care of that guilt for you when He died on the cross. And when memories of shame hit you because of things your abuser said to you, or because you are embarrassed that you allowed yourself to be in the relationship or stay in it so long, remember that Jesus also scorned shame on that cross for you. He scorned it for the *"joy"* set *before Him*, and that joy set before Him was us.

Finally, I want to encourage you to release any pain you are still feeling to God. Just give it to Him. Ask God to take away your pain and help you rebuild, restore, and renew your mind so you can reclaim your true identity in Christ. Take what He says in the Bible to heart. Write down all of the positive qualities you have and look at them each day. Remind yourself of how God sees you.

Just as you internalized all of the nasty and hurtful things your abuser tried to convince you of during your relationship, you now need to re-train your mind and internalize the things God says about you and that you know to be true. It may take time to feel better about yourself, but once you do, you will be ready for your final challenge, which is to forgive your abuser.

12

Working Toward Forgiveness

This is the chapter I had the most difficulty writing and it will probably be the chapter you have the most difficulty reading. It certainly will be the subject you will probably wrestle with the most. And that's ok, because at one time, I had to wrestle with it too. The idea of forgiving the person who abused you and caused you so much pain might seem daunting and perhaps even horrific at first. You may be nowhere close to being ready to even consider forgiving your abuser. And that's ok too.

My goal is to not only lay the groundwork and equip you with everything you should consider before making your decision, but to also give you the ability to do so when you are ready to do it. There is absolutely no need to rush the process. Everyone who has survived an abusive relationship is on their own journey of discovery and timeline for healing. The main goal here is to just keep making progress at your own pace until you finally get there.

One of the problems most survivors of abuse have with the idea of forgiveness is that we think it will force us to ignore the fact that someone we deeply loved at one time, hurt us so bad. We often feel the need to be an advocate for ourselves by angrily reminding ourselves and the rest of the world of the injustice that was committed against us. In fact, forgiveness is often considered the F-word to those who have been abused. That's because it feels empowering when we are angry, and the idea of letting go of something which makes us feel empowered is a somewhat scary thought.

Is forgiveness really necessary for healing? I realize that many people reading this will absolutely cringe at the idea. But the short answer is absolutely yes. I'm not saying that it will be easy to get to the point of being able to do so, but it is so worth it when you finally can. I am also *not* suggesting that at some point you discuss or share your decision to forgive with your abuser. This is about your healing not theirs, and they have no need to know anything about your personal healing from their abuse. Hopefully this facet of the process just made the whole concept of forgiving your abuser more palatable to consider.

While there are many benefits to forgiveness, the main one is freedom - the freedom of letting go. When you lay down your rights for justice, fairness, and restitution, you are giving yourself the gift of freedom. Studies have also shown that forgiveness can result in huge health benefits like reducing the risk of heart attack, improving cholesterol levels, increasing your quality of sleep, reducing pain, lowering blood pressure, along with reducing levels of anxiety, depression and stress. In fact, I would argue that the mental and physical health benefits alone make the act of forgiveness worth considering.

That said, there are elements that can keep you from forgiving your abuser, especially from *fully* forgiving. At the time you finally summoned up the courage to leave them, there was probably no conceivable way that you could imagine ever being able to forgive your abuser. After all, this is a person who committed a crime(s) against you so evil and horrific that it would probably seem foolish for you to even consider forgiving them. It may not be easy, but no matter how badly you have been hurt, your ability to forgive will

definitely help you to heal regardless of how it impacts your abuser.
Before I go on, I want to dispel a few myths and wrong beliefs about
forgiving your abuser:

- **Forgiveness doesn't mean it was okay.**
  - » You are not condoning what happened or saying you de-
    served it. You are fully recognizing the wrongness of what
    was done and placing the blame on the other person.
- **Forgiveness is not a statement that the crime was not
  that bad.**
  - » You still feel the wounds that were inflicted on you, and
    you will probably carry some of the scars for life.
- **Forgiveness is not something you do to avoid feeling
  the impact of the damage.**
  - » You are simply choosing to let the offense(s) go and giving
    them back to your abuser. You are returning the "gift" they
    gave you so it can no longer impact your life.
- **Forgiveness doesn't mean you won't hurt.**
  - » You will still feel some emotion at times from what you
    lost, what you miss, and what could have been. It will still
    affect you at times, just not as bad.
- **Forgiveness is not the same as forgetting.**
  - » Just because you forgive someone, doesn't mean you sud-
    denly gain amnesia. You may never forget what happened
    to you.
- **Forgiveness is not something anyone can force upon
  you.**
  - » Every survivor that wrestles with the idea of forgiving their
    abuser has to come to their decision on their own timeline
    and comfort level.
- **Forgiveness is not giving lip service.**
  - » Your forgiveness has to be genuine toward your abuser. It
    has to be something you truly want to do in order to have
    the releasing and cleansing effect for your recovery.

- **Forgiveness has nothing to do with fairness.**
  - » Letting go of the pain and anger you feel doesn't change the fact that the abusive behavior was wrong. It's about you having the power to forgive in order to prioritize *your* healing.
- **Forgiveness isn't about letting your abuser off the hook.**
  - » Forgiveness is not declaring that what has happened to you is ok, nor does it mean that the abuse was your fault. Your abuser will still have to deal with the ramifications of their actions.
- **Forgiveness doesn't require an apology from your abuser.**
  - » Forgiveness is the personal process of you voluntarily deciding to let go of your anger, resentment, and thoughts of revenge. It requires no apology before you can forgive.

It is important to understand that forgiveness is not a feeling you wait to suddenly have. It is a decision you arrive at that says despite what this person has done to you, and how you feel about them, you're choosing to forgive them for what they have done. That's not an easy decision to arrive at. While part of you may want to forgive, another part of you may strongly resist doing so. A part of you might want to still hold onto not forgiving as a weapon or a shield against being hurt again. And that's completely understandable because your mind still remembers what it felt like while you were being abused. But you have a far greater understanding of what happened to you now and many more skills that you can utilize to protect yourself, so you need to assure that part of you that it is going to be ok.

Even with the best intentions, you need to realize that forgiving your abuser is a process that takes time to come to terms with. It simply doesn't happen overnight. There are a lot of aspects to the abuse you experienced that you need to deal with and ultimately forgive. You are growing every day, and the more you fully understand not just who, but what you are forgiving, the easier it will be to reach a decision to do so. There are a number of steps you should consider taking that can help you reach that decision.

If you haven't already, it is very important to recognize and face the abuse that was committed against you. As time passes by and more distance is placed between when the abuse occurred and where you are now, you may be tempted to rationalize it away or minimize its impact on your life. But that's just a way of masking or burying the pain you felt at the time. I'd like to encourage you to write a list of everything your abuser did to hurt you. Yes, it is a record of wrongs to the best of your recollection, but you are only keeping it temporarily. Its purpose is to help you look at your abuser squarely in the eyes and then let their offenses go.

Behind each offense committed by your abuser are the emotions that those offenses triggered. Take the time and think about how each offense or action made you feel. Write those feelings down next to each offense. Did you feel anger, shame, betrayal, hatred, humiliation, confusion etc.? What impact have those offenses and subsequent attached emotions had on your life? Are you still feeling those same emotions or are you able to just look back on them and acknowledge them? Look at your feelings of resentment, resistance, and anger regarding the idea of forgiving your abuser as well. If you haven't dealt with them yet, find ways to release those emotions. Talk about them with someone, cry, scream or write about them. Pray to God about them and release them to Him.

At some point, when you're ready, you will finally arrive at the decision to let it all go—your abuser, their offenses and the feelings that went with them. When you do this, you are making a conscious decision to surrender your right to hold your offender accountable, *forever*. Let go of the need to want them to change, the need for them to apologize, the need for others to see, the need for others to know, the wounds you still feel, everything. Let-it-all-go.

In his beautiful book *Restored,* author Neil T. Anderson has a wonderful, simple method and prayer he suggests for forgiving your abuser (or anyone for that matter):

*Lord, I choose to forgive (<u>name of the person</u>), For (<u>what they did</u>
<u>to you</u>), Which made me feel (<u>share the painful memories</u>)*

*Lord Jesus, I choose not to hold on to my resentment and bitterness.
I relinquish my right to seek revenge and I ask you to heal my damaged emotions. Thank You for setting me free from the bondage of
bitterness and free from my past experiences. I now ask you to bless
this person who has hurt me. In Jesus' name I pray. Amen.*

Most people who have experienced emotional abuse will encounter
new memories of old violations from time to time, along with the
emotions that those memories trigger. As the saying goes, abuse is
the gift that keeps on giving. Yes, you absolutely have the right to experience whatever emotions you feel and then to express them. But I
want to encourage you to go through this process and pray this prayer
every time a new memory of an offense comes to your mind. Think
about it for a few minutes, process *how* it makes you feel and *why* it
makes you feel that way. Then release it and let it go.

The Bible gives us another very important reason to forgive. We forgive others because God forgave us. Ephesians 4:32 says:

*"Be kind and compassionate to one another, forgiving each other,
just as in Christ God forgave you."*

When you take the time to think about how much God has forgiven
you, it will cause you to be more forgiving of those who have hurt you.
God has completely wiped your sin slate clean because of what Jesus
Christ did on the cross. Everything you deserve to be paid back for in
life has been cleared away because God has forgiven you. When you
apply that statement for yourself, I hope you'll find it increasingly tough
to hold a grudge against someone else, even your abuser.

There's also a major benefit to releasing offenses as they come to mind
and living a life in forgiveness. It prevents those offensive memories

from residing in your mind and clouding up your thinking. You no longer need to rehearse the crimes committed against you over and over in your head. You are no longer allowing your abuser to occupy and control your primary thoughts. You are giving yourself the ability to live free from the captivity of needing to hold another person accountable forever. You are giving yourself the freedom to let go.

13

Understanding Your Abuser

One of the challenges that we abuse survivors have to deal with that impedes our desire and ability to forgive our abusers, is that we usually can't see them any other way except as abusive. We may have little understanding of what made them the monsters they are. Yes, abuse is a choice and emotional abusers are fully aware of what they are doing, but most of their behavior was learned from growing up in dysfunctional and unstable environments as a child. They weren't just born with the behavior.

Abusers and people with Cluster B disorders often come from families where their parents have very unhealthy and toxic relationships. There's often a lot of fighting, substance abuse and infidelity going on by one or both parents and the children are caught in between, watching all of it unfold and subconsciously picking up the toxic behavior. They often will develop unhealthy coping mechanisms to deal with all of the vitriol and emotional vomit that is spewed around the household.

The parents will often turn their abuse and anger toward their children and this abuse from the child's parents often continues into their adult lives. The children get used to being talked down to and insulted by the adult figures in their lives from whom they desperately want to receive love, and so they try to find approval from other people which in turn can lead to an unhealthy desire for attention and affection. They develop unhealthy and dysfunctional ways to get what they want, no matter who else it hurts along the way. Childhood sexual trauma also plays a role in the development of Cluster B disorders.

Findings from the Collaborative Longitudinal Personality Disorders Study found a definitive link between the number and type of child-hood traumas and the development of personality disorders. In many cases the children suffered from verbal abuse from one or both of their parents, and it was especially damaging if the verbal abuse came from the mother. The study found that children who were screamed at, told that they weren't loved, or threatened to be sent away by their mothers were three times as likely to have borderline, narcissistic, ob-sessive-compulsive or paranoid disorders in adulthood compared to children raised in healthy families.

I mention all of this because I want to point out that people aren't just born with Cluster B disorders; they develop them in response to trauma. Yes, there is some research that genetics play a small role in some of the Cluster B personality disorders especially antisocial disorder (ASPD). But for the most part, abusers were initially victims of their childhood. They had no control over their living conditions and they didn't pick out their parents. They didn't choose to be men-tally, physically or sexually abused, belittled, neglected or abandoned by those same parents. They didn't choose to watch them cheat, fight, yell, get drunk, take drugs or never be at home.

Sometimes other environmental factors come into play. Some parents can be at the other extreme end of the spectrum and never provide any constructive criticism, discipline or appropriate punishment when it is called for. They may only provide positive reinforcement when the child completes certain approved behaviors, occasionally fawning on the child excessively at times and ignoring them the rest. This all leads to more confusion about what types of behavior will earn the approval of their parents and ultimately, society at large. Meanwhile the child has no one to help them learn how to cope with the stress of growing up.

Now take this one step further. The child is now an adult and brings the only behaviors they know into their relationships. They have come to believe that not only is abusive behavior and fighting acceptable, but they now use it to maintain control in their relationships. Their need for survival and dysfunctional training to get attention and the things they desperately want or need develops them into experts in the art of deception and manipulation. They become so laser focused on the end result, that they have no ability to consider the needs or feeling of others in their quest to achieve that result.

The Four Cluster B Disorders

Unfortunately, this type of person came into your relationship severely damaged emotionally and mentally from toxic, dysfunctional families and childhood experiences, abuse and previous bad and hurtful relationships. These experiences often create responses in those hurt individuals that lead to them developing one or more of the four Cluster B disorders that include Borderline Personality Disorder (BPD), Narcissistic Personality Disorder (NPD), Histrionic Personality Disorder (HPD), and Antisocial Personality Disorder (ASPD). Add to this other disorders like Obsessive Compulsive Disorder (OCD), and you have a volatile cocktail of dysfunction that can not only kill a marriage or relationship, but cause extreme damage to the person or people (spouses, children, friends) they purport to love. As the saying goes: "hurt people, hurt people." Most often, it's the ones closest to them.

All of the Cluster B disorders are characterized by dramatic, inappropriate, volatile emotions and unpredictable, erratic, impulsive and manipulative behavior. While there are four distinct disorders, and they can each occur on their own, the people who suffer from them often have overlapping symptoms. All of the personality disorders are deeply ingrained, rigid ways of behaving that affect that person's relationships as well as their mental well-being.

Although their actual, deep-seated personal distress may not be visible to us very often, the harmful coping strategies a Cluster B uses against us are. Regardless of the specific type(s) of disorder the person you were involved with or married to suffered from, you must understand that the disorders are a mental health condition that affects the way the person thinks, behaves and relates to others.

The behavior of a person with one or more of the four Cluster B Disorders can be best characterized as someone who has difficulty regulating their emotions. This leads to consistent, long-term and un-healthy patterns of thinking, feeling and behaving. Personality disorders are difficult to cure because the people who suffer from them often have abnormal thoughts and behaviors that prevent them from think-ing and functioning the way they should. This in turn makes it difficult for them to accept that they are actually suffering from a disorder that is harming them and causing an incredible amount of emotional (and sometimes physical) damage to those around them.

I share all this because sometimes the only way we can get to a point of forgiveness with our abusers is to see them from a different per-spective. For me, the ability to let go and forgive came from the reality that, while my abuser was responsible for all of the physical and emo-tional pain that she inflicted on me (consciously and subconsciously), much of what she did to me was deeply rooted in a past she initially had no control over. Yes, she absolutely is responsible for everything she has ever done in her life, especially in actions and offenses she has committed against myself and other people. But I had to ask myself, if I had been placed in the exact circumstances from childhood on, who's to say that I would have turned out any differently?

But I want to make it clear that forgiving does not mean excusing. What was done to you was beyond wrong and there will never be any acceptable excuse for it. This is strictly to give you perspective and help you gain complete freedom from your abuser. Many people including myself, have witnessed toxic dysfunction in their own families and didn't become abusers.

No matter where or from what they develop their behavior, people who commit abuse make a choice in doing so. They could also choose not to. Every survivor of emotional abuse has now been exposed to it. We can use our experience to end the cycle of abuse, heal ourselves and share our experience to help others instead of causing further harm to other people because of what we experienced.

Because if a disorder or behavior can be developed and adopted, it can also be addressed, regulated, moderated, healed or removed from that person's life with the help of counseling, therapy and a lot of work and desire on the part of the person with the disorder. But they have to want to do it. And until they choose to acknowledge and face their own toxic behavior and become committed to long-term therapy, they will continue to be a human wrecking ball in the lives of everyone they encounter, especially those that they claim to love.

Your abuser's past will catch up with them at some point. They can only hide and run away from their insecurities, failures, lies and dysfunction for so long. Everything comes to light eventually, and all will be revealed. God is watching and knows and sees all things. He will be the ultimate judge of them in the end.

14

Forgiving Yourself

If you are still having trouble forgiving your abuser it might be because there is one other person you also need to forgive, and that is yourself. That's because most abuse survivors often feel guilt, shame and self-blame in four areas: 1) For allowing ourselves to get into the relationship in the first place, 2) not noticing or ignoring all of the warning signs of our abuser's future behavior, 3) for tolerating the actual abuse, and 4) then staying in the relationship for as long as we did. Now add to that the friends and family members we pushed away or became isolated from all in the name of love for our abuser, or any guilt we may feel for the times we might have reacted angrily toward our abuser and we have a lot to be angry about against ourselves.

Self-blame is a common component among survivors of all types of abuse, including emotional abuse. That's because it feels like there is no other way to explain the extreme dysfunctional behavior we "chose" to put up with from the very person who was supposed to love and cherish us. On top of this, society often adds to the shame we feel, as if we have committed the terrible crime of being a victim. Abuse is never our fault, but you wouldn't know it by the way society often frowns upon and shuns survivors of abuse, as if we're defective for having been targeted by our abuser in the first place.

We live in a victim-blaming society that gaslights us into believing that we have to be responsible for "our part" for something that was done *to* us. Sadly, this victim-shaming narrative is deeply embedded in every aspect of our society and its effect is often to completely invalidate the abuse we experienced. Sure, your abuser was absolutely horrible, but the abuse you experienced would never have happened if you hadn't placed yourself in a relationship with them in the first place, right?

We also experience our own form of toxic shame that comes from the deep-seated trauma we have experienced. The lovely, wonderful effect of that trauma is that it can wear you down with shame and make you feel as if you need to justify, apologize, and overextend yourself in explaining what happened to you and why you did what you did. The end result is that it can make you feel as if you aren't good enough. And then you start to internalize all of this self-blame and its starts to feel like you are interrogating yourself.

And the questions you ask yourself are endless:

- How could I have been so naïve?
- Why didn't I notice the warning signs?
- Why didn't I listen to my friends and family?
- Why didn't I stand up for myself more/better?
- Why did I tolerate the abuse?
- How did I allow myself to become a victim?
- Why did I hide the abuse from everyone?
- Why did I protect and cover for my abuser?
- Why didn't I leave sooner?
- What's wrong with me?

And in the midst of all this self-blaming and self-interrogation we often lose sight of all of the actual things that kept us from doing the very things we are questioning ourselves about. We forget that we didn't throw in the towel right away because we had empathy for our abuser's personal history and previous experiences. We continued to love them and tried to help them. We often overlook the fact that we had fully invested ourselves in the relationship. We forget about the blowups, backlash, shunning and numerous other silencing tactics we endured throughout the relationship when we did fight back or defend ourselves.

All of this unhealthy self-blame requires that we reframe the questions we ask ourselves and with which we allow society to frame us. And it makes self-forgiveness a crucial step in our personal healing process. You have to realize that the sense of blame you may be feeling does not actually belong to you. It lies with the person who committed crimes against you and often created events and placed you in situations that were beyond your control. All you could do was respond or react. You did not choose or set out to be emotionally abused. So, let's re-visit some aspects of the relationship to remind you of this fact and the natural humanity that exists inside of you.

First of all, you have to get to a point in which it is ok to admit that you were seriously misled and duped. Your abuser offered up and presented a version of themselves that mirrored and exploited all of your best qualities. In a very real sense, you fell in love with yourself. You thought the two of you were becoming soulmates of the highest order. It felt deep and real, as if all of the planets had aligned to create the most incredible bonding experience between two people in the history of mankind. And you made a decision to enter into a relationship with them based on the information given to you at the time, and you had no reason to believe otherwise.

The reality is that you had no idea that your abuser was looking for someone with the exact amazing qualities you possessed. It wasn't a cosmic, supernatural accident. The moment they met you, they set into motion a plan to take advantage of all that you offered – love, affection, compassion, empathy, financial stability, honesty, respect and trustworthiness. Qualities which would absolutely flourish in healthier situations, with healthier, like-minded people.

You checked off all the boxes in their criteria list of a perfect future victim. You became idealized by them and it felt truly amazing. You had no idea someone else, quite inhumane and evil could exist inside of the same person with whom you fell in love. You had no idea that your abuser didn't have the capability to actually feel genuine love or show authentic emotion because they were just a shell of a normal human being.

Once you fell deeply in love with them and became fully committed to the relationship, your abuser started the devaluing process by slowly and deliberately pointing out all of the shortcomings *they* saw in you. They trained you how to question yourself and everything you did, said and even thought. They started conditioning you to tiptoe and walk on eggshells around them, so you were never sure of how they would behave toward you next. They taught you that their phony love and affection now had to be earned and when you did, you probably didn't deserve it and you should have been thankful for the love scraps they did throw your way.

When things started to go sideways and your abuser started acting up, the first thing in your mind wasn't to jump ship on the relationship. You naturally tried harder to make your abuser happy. You still had hope that things could get better because *you* possessed the ability to genuinely love. You made the conscious decision to endure the abuse because you believed things could improve and also because your abuser most likely constantly reminded you that if only you didn't fall short in so many areas, then they would indeed be happy and the abuse would stop. You had hope because that's what *real* love does; it hopes.

You persevered and you plowed forward with hope for better days ahead. And then your abuser turned up the heat. He/she told you how worthless they thought you were, started calling you names, gaslighting you, manipulating you, ignoring you, isolating you and ultimately confusing you. You started to see their true colors, and responded by calling attention to their abusive behavior and how it made you feel. You may have even found the strength to suggest counseling for them or the both of you together. Then they started threatening you in different ways that made you question leaving them and consider what the fallout would be if you did.

Eventually you found the strength to leave them. It may have been one particular event that pushed you over the top or just a culmination of the unbearable pain you endured and finally had enough of. And now you are left holding an empty bag that once held all of your deepest hopes, dreams and desires. Not only have they been left unfulfilled, but you now wonder whether you contributed to the bag being empty. But just because you wanted to be in a loving relationship and stayed longer than you should have, doesn't mean you deserved to be abused.

There may also have been times, especially toward the end of the relationship, when you responded to your abuser in ways that you aren't especially proud of. You may be feeling guilty about that too. But it's important to understand that you aren't remotely on the same level as your emotional abuser. You didn't carefully stage your angry response(s) with the mission to reassert your power and control over the relationship. You didn't explode to cause maximum damage to your partner. You just desperately wanted to stand up for yourself and be heard. You just were at your wits end and couldn't take it anymore. The fact that you even remotely feel remorseful for your response shows how different you are from your abuser.

You are not to blame for being groomed by your abusive predator or for being taken advantage of by someone you trusted. After all, your abuser didn't unmask their true intentions for power and control over you until you were already fully invested in the relationship. You just happened to place your trust in a truly skilled manipulator who was an expert in the art of deception. And now they have left you with a final parting gift of questioning yourself and wondering if you were partly to blame for their actions. You may feel like you have left the warzone with your abuser and stepped into a war within yourself.

In hindsight, you may well have stayed longer than you should have, but your circumstances are unique to you, and for a number of reasons you didn't leave as soon as you should have and that's ok. There are a lot of things to consider before leaving any relationship, especially an abusive one. There may be children, financial considerations, moving, settling in a new location and even getting used to the inevitability of being alone again.

You stayed in your abusive relationship because of the trauma you received and endured, not because you lacked intelligence, strength or character. The trauma you experienced was not your fault. You didn't deserve to be emotionally abused, verbally assaulted or taken advantage of. What matters is that *you finally did get out*. What matters is you won't go back to your abuser and their toxic dysfunction, and you won't allow anyone else to treat you that way again going forward. You genuinely loved your abuser, and the relationship failed in spite of your efforts. Now it's time to pick up the pieces of your life and learn to love and trust again. And that process starts with forgiving yourself.

All of us have a critical voice inside of our heads that narrates our every move. No one beats us up better than we can beat up ourselves. It's the old "if only" could've, should've, would've syndrome. When we make a mistake or do something we regret, we connect those things to the feelings they trigger, which are actually the root causes of what is holding us back from healing emotionally.

When we try to forgive ourselves, what we're really trying to do is release something that *feels* like it is a part of us. But what we are releasing is actually a part of our past that isn't essentially who we are *unless* we have built our identity around it. In most cases, had we known the things that were going to happen to us, we would have avoided them, right? But they did happen, they were real and they mattered. And you did the best you could under the circumstances at the time they happened.

None of us asked for the hurt, the shame, the embarrassment or the regret that comes from being abused. So often, we don't really know what to do with these underlying feelings and confused emotions; we just know we don't like them. And when our abuser doesn't offer an apology to make us feel better, all we can do is retain what we learned from the experience and release the rest of it.

In order to forgive ourselves, it is imperative that we come to the understanding that we could never have prevented what happened to us from happening. With foresight or hindsight, we might have been able to *avoid* it, but we certainly couldn't have prevented it from happening because we didn't know it was going to happen. And the truth is, abuse can happen to anyone, anyplace at anytime.

If you think about it, when we forgive others, we usually do it from a place of love. In fact, we tend to forgive others to the degree that we love them. We often refer back to the love and goodness we see in them, in order to forgive them. So, let me ask you two questions: Do you love yourself? Don't you think you are worthy of being loved? The problem is that we often don't have the same love for ourselves as we do for others. In fact, we are usually harder on ourselves. I know I am. We give other people the benefit of the doubt, but we don't cut ourselves any slack at all. Acknowledge your suffering, scream at it and wrestle with it if you have to, and then remind yourself that you didn't cause it.

I want you to consider giving yourself a pardon because you need to stop punishing yourself for something that was out of your control and for which you were not responsible. It's time to have some compassion for yourself. You don't have to carry the blame that rightfully rests on the shoulders of your abuser. The important thing is never how long you stay in an abusive relationship; it's that you find the strength to leave in the end. Forgive yourself not only for having those angry feelings but also for struggling to let go of those feelings. What matters isn't where you are or where you were; what matters is where you are going. You have the rest of your life ahead of you and you have so much more to do with it!

15

What God Thinks about Abuse

I often get a number of questions from people who ask me about my faith in Jesus despite the horrible emotional abuse I incurred. They wonder how I can believe in a God who they believe just stood by while I suffered. The three questions I get the most regardless of whether the person believes in God or not are:

1. Where was God during my abuse?
2. Why didn't He do anything about it?
3. What does God think about abuse?

I believe these questions are important especially when abuse victims are members of a church whose pastors or leadership incorrectly instruct them to stay in their marriage despite the abuse. But these are fair questions for anyone to ask, especially when someone has just spent months or years being emotionally abused and is seeking comfort from a God they can't see. I will do my best to answer these questions and others you might have, the way I have personally experienced these very thoughts while I was being abused, and then subsequently had during my recovery.

First of all, let me just say that contrary to anything you may have read or been incorrectly taught, God doesn't set up children, women or men to be abused in any shape or form. God doesn't perpetrate abuse on His Creation. Fallen, broken human beings do that all on their own. God doesn't control people. He has given people freewill and allowed them to make their own decisions dating all the way back to the Garden of Eden with Adam and Eve, and He has let every human ever since that time make their own decisions and choices in life. People sin, and they do horrible things to other people. We live in a world where suffering happens and we can see the effects of this all around us.

But Jesus has experienced what we have at the hands of the very same people. He was betrayed, beaten, ridiculed, and ultimately murdered to bear our sins on the cross. The Bible says in Luke 22:44 that Jesus was so stressed and anguished before he was betrayed that:

> "His sweat was like drops of blood falling to the ground".

Jesus was a man of sorrows who was acquainted with our grief. Isaiah 53: 3-5 describes Jesus this way:

> "He was despised and rejected by mankind, a man of suffering, and familiar with pain. Like one from whom people hide their faces he was despised, and we held him in low esteem. Surely he took up our pain and bore our suffering, yet we considered him punished by God, stricken by him, and afflicted. But he was pierced for our transgressions, he was crushed for our iniquities; the punishment that brought us peace was on him, and by his wounds we are healed."

This Scripture shows us that Jesus truly felt these things, and that what He felt went well beyond mere emotions or shallow sentimentality. This is a reminder that He cares and that He carries our burdens. In fact, there are three times in Scripture that Jesus wept (John 11:35, Luke 19:41 and Hebrews 5:7-9). Each moment is near the end of His life and reveals what matters most to Him.

Hebrews 4:15 describes Jesus as someone who is truly touched with the feeling of our infirmities. His tears serve as a reminder that He loves and cares for all of us. Nowhere is this more evident than when he died on the cross for us. And I believe that this is where He was while you and I were being abused. He was weeping on the cross and reliving His crucifixion. He was looking at us, grieving for us and shaking his head in compassion as He saw us betrayed by the very person that we believed He brought into our life—the person that was supposed to love us, care for us, respect us, honor us and most importantly, protect us. And He wept.

When we are hurting or grieving a significant loss, it is completely human to wonder if God is watching or listening. We may want to clench our fists and scream in agony, "*Lord, do you hear my cries?*" There are times when you may feel that no one including God will understand, let alone have sympathy for what you are going through. I fully can relate to someone who has cried themselves to sleep at night. That's what abuse of any kind can do to you. And the nights seem endless. You pray for the ability to fall asleep so you can temporarily forget what your abuser has done to you that day and how much they've hurt you. The hopelessness you continually feel can be excruciating.

But Jesus can relate to you because he has felt what you have felt and are feeling. I truly believe he was there with me during my time of pain and grief because His Word tells me so. Psalm 34:17-18 says:

> "*The righteous call to the Lord, and he listens; he rescues them from all their troubles. The Lord is near to those who are discouraged; he saves those who have lost all hope.*"

And He did, and I'm alive today because He gave me hope, a vision for my future without my abuser, and the strength to leave my abuser. Jesus is in the business of helping us pick up the pieces, get healed, and get on with our lives. Psalm 40:1-2 says:

"I waited patiently for the Lord's help; then he listened to me and heard my cry. He set me safely on a rock and made me secure."

At the heart of all the amazing things that God is, He's a rescuer. He knows what we are feeling and He doesn't want us to continue being filled with sadness and grief because we cannot save our relationship and bear another day of pain and abuse. God's heart is always for us, whenever we are being harmed, and no matter what type of abuse we are experiencing. He sees that our souls are aching from pain and he sees the damage that the emotional abuse is having on our minds and bodies. He knows that the anxiety, depression and PTSD we are experiencing is as painful and harder to treat than many physical injuries. God sees our suffering for what it is and he sees it with love and compassion for us. He doesn't want us to suffer. God promises to love us, to be with us, to assist us in our efforts to overcome the effects of sin here on earth, and to one day set us free for all eternity.

What God Thinks about Abuse

No matter what weapons an abuser uses, they attack the image of God (you) and they war against Him. Because an abuser is separated from God by their actions, they cannot see what God sees in us. When your abuser wages war on you, they are waging war against God. They are ignoring the fact that we are deeply loved by God and that we have been redeemed *by* Him at a great cost *to* Him. Every time an abuser attacks, insults, controls, manipulates and hurts us, God sees and knows that they are stealing the liberty and peace He provides for us. They are coming against and violating God's sacred commitment to love, honor and protect us.

And make no mistake, God sees every underhanded moment of abuse, every theft of property, every manipulation, every insult, each instant of gaslighting and every lie in every place and every time they occur. What you feel, He feels, and when your abuser comes against you, they come against Him. Whether we (or your abuser) realize it or not, God is standing next to us, watching as each unpleasant and painful event is unfolding. He sees the heart of evil that is inside of each abuser and he feels the struggle and brokenness of every victim. He sees your broken heart, your disbelief and your constant hope that what you are experiencing won't continue.

And whether you think so or not, it was actually God's voice whispering in your ear which made you aware that you were actually being abused. It was God who taught you to identify the abusive behaviors for what they were and realize they weren't fair, right or deserved. It was God who helped you to see and understand the deceitfulness, control and manipulation behind every accusation, insult, lie, gaslighting, shunning, and silent treatment committed against you. It was God who opened your eyes and convinced you it was time to flee your abuser. It was God who helped you to see the truth and gave you the courage to leave your abuser and that awful situation.

God saw that even when you were being abused, you still had empathy for your abuser and tried to save your relationship. He saw the strength you had as you tolerated the abuse, hoping to make things better. He watched as you hopelessly tried to love and help your abuser all while trying to find answers and solutions to their toxic dysfunction, despite their constant abuse and quest to control and manipulate you.

But biblical love does not help an abuser or try to keep them comfortable while they are trying to harm us and tear us apart at the seams. Biblical love actually requires accountability and justice, whether we ever set foot in a court of law or simply flee the abusive relationship and distance ourselves from our abuser. In fact, God tells us in Leviticus 5:1 that it is actually a sin not to bring someone's sins against another human being or God to public light. God also tells us what He thinks about abuse.

God hates abuse.

"There are six things that the Lord hates, seven that are an abomination to him: haughty eyes, a lying tongue, and hands that shed innocent blood, a heart that devises wicked plans, feet that make haste to run to evil, a false witness who breathes out lies, and one who sows discord among brothers." (Proverbs 6:16-19)

God says verbal (emotional) abuse harms people and carries the power of death.

"Death and life are in the power of the tongue." (Proverbs 18:21)

God says emotional abuse is a heavy burden to bear up under.

"A stone is heavy, and sand a burden, but provocation by a fool is heavier than both." (Proverbs 27:3)

"A man's spirit will endure sickness, but a crushed spirit who can bear?" (Proverbs 18:14)

God says verbal (emotional) abuse is the equivalent of being gutted with a knife.

"Reckless words pierce like a sword, but the tongue of the wise brings healing." (Proverbs 12:18)

God says an abuser is a fraud, and their religion is worthless.

"If anyone thinks he is religious and does not bridle his tongue but deceives his heart, this person's religion is worthless." (James 1:26)

God's response to abuse is reflected in His strong statement in Malachi 2:16 that says

"I hate a man's covering himself with violence as well as with his garment says the Lord Almighty."

For a man or woman to cover their garment with wrong, symbolizes both the action of violence and an abusive inner state, which violates the covenant of marriage. But this could be applied to any relationship. Ultimately, abuse perverts the image of God. What should be a state of mutual encouragement, support, nurturing, sustaining and enhancing each partner's need for love and affection, abuse destroys it. It goes against the basic human function to care for God's creation.

One of the final obstacles and perhaps the greatest to our emotional wholeness and full healing is the lack of fairness that we often feel about our abuser not being held accountable or exposed for who they really are and going free. But God promises that judgment will eventually be done. Nahum 1:2-3 says:

"The Lord takes vengeance on His foes and maintains his wrath against his enemies. The Lord is slow to anger and great in power; the Lord will not leave the guilty unpunished."

God will deal with our abusers according to the crimes they have committed against us. Of that you can be certain. This is why we can forgive our abuser without surrendering justice. No matter what your abuser has done to you, it will not go unpunished. Because God will ultimately have the last word.

16

Being Intentional about Your Healing

It's easy to get stuck focusing on your relationship or marriage while you are in the middle of the turmoil caused by your abuser's toxic behavior. At the time it is happening, you bounce between coping and licking your wounds; to trying to get them to change, stop abusing you, or get them the help they so desperately need. A toxic relationship requires your undivided attention just to survive each day of abusive behavior.

These survival techniques and coping mechanisms become so ingrained in our day to day living, that when we realize they are not going to make a difference in our relationship or our abuser, a sense of discouragement and depression can sink in. I distinctly remember the feeling of hopelessness I had when I realized that all of the energy I had invested trying to save my relationship had been a waste of time, and that I was powerless to save it.

There comes a moment when the reality that you can't get your abuser to change and that you can't help to heal your abusive marriage or relationship finally sinks in. It's a tough nut to swallow especially when your abuser continues to choose to abuse you. Having given it your best shot, you now realize that you have to step away and leave the relationship forever because you won't be able to survive if you stay in that situation any longer.

Once you make that decision, it's imperative that you turn all of the focus you had on your abuser and the relationship, toward yourself. It's time to stop paying attention to what your abuser is doing and wondering and waiting to see if they will change, and, instead, putting all of your energy into your needs, recovery and healing. It's imperative to invest your time, energy and emotions in yourself from this point forward.

You will soon find that it is easier and more constructive to focus on your own healing and creating your new life, than to try to wonder how you might still fix your abuser's personality disorders. And yet, you may still be tempted to occasionally see what they are doing or wonder how they are responding to your decision. Don't. It's just a distraction and it takes much needed attention away from the person that needs it the most, which is you.

Once you leave, you have to stop looking back. This is your time, so take advantage of it and don't let thoughts about your abuser and what they might be thinking or doing distract you. You need to focus on the very real damage that the abuse has done to you. You need time to re-discover the things in your life you can take back control of and regain your sense of self again. There are going to be times that you might get discouraged and your mind may wonder, but just stay focused on your healing and realize it is something you absolutely do have influence over and control of.

Don't Stay Stuck in the Past

There is a time when you first leave your abuser, are in the middle of moving out, working through a divorce or just trying to get settled into your new life, when it is truly important to talk about your abuser and understand the abuse you were exposed to and endlessly endured.

There is a place for this, especially when it helps you process your anger and other feelings you've had pent up inside of you, and when you are still trying to land on your feet again.

While it's only natural to think about the past or what could have been, and wondering if your abuser is going to keep getting away with their toxic and dysfunctional behavior, or if they are going to find someone else to hurt, that's not where your focus should be. That's because the answer to those thoughts and questions are not going to help you get better. They aren't going to add any value to your life going forward.

Think about this for a moment. How does knowing what your abuser is thinking or saying about you going to help you heal? If anything, it will only hurt you or make you angry again. How does knowing if they are in a new relationship or possibly abusing someone else make you feel better? It will probably just trigger anger or jealousy and make you feel you weren't good enough. To truly heal, you have to turn your attention off of your abuser and onto you. Your healing process absolutely has to be all about you, not them.

Intentional Faithfulness

As you have probably discovered by now, you don't just automatically heal after you leave your abusive relationship. You can't just wave a magic wand, gulp a panacea drink and make all of the brokenness go away. Most survivors (including myself) are emotionally exhausted and absolutely overwhelmed by what we have just gone through and what it is going to take to rebuild our torn-up lives.

And while I'm a big believer in what God can do in our lives and the power we have to heal in Him, we can't just offer up a prayer and hope that God takes all of our problems away. We can't just wait for and expect Jesus to do everything for us. We have to be intentional and take personal responsibility for our healing, using the tools He gives us and the people He puts in our lives to help us to make progress in our healing. As the saying goes, "God gives worms for birds to eat, but He doesn't put them in their nests." This is another way to say that we need to walk in what I call intentional faithfulness.

There are three quick stories in the Bible that I want to share with you that illustrate the concept of intentional faithfulness. In Matthew 8:1-3 Jesus is coming down from the mountainside after preaching to crowds all day long. The Bible tells us that:

> "A man with leprosy came and knelt before him and said, Lord, if you are willing, you can make me clean. Jesus reached out his hand and touched the man. 'I am willing', he said. 'Be clean!' Immediately he was cured of his leprosy."

On the surface of this story, it seems like all the leper had to do was ask Jesus to heal him. But you need to know the incredible effort it took for the leper just to get to Jesus. Leprosy puts a person in indescribable shame and misery. A leper was highly contagious and most people would have scorned the man because leprosy was considered a sign of uncleanness, a mark of God's displeasure and that person was considered unfit to worship God.

Lepers in those days were truly despised. He would have been separated from his family and friends. He would have been an outcast, isolated from other people. Roadway travel was not permitted for lepers, so his access would have been much harder to get to Jesus. On top of all that, he probably was filled with alienation and shame because of what the rest of society felt about him. And yet he made the effort to see Jesus and was cured. He walked with intentional faithfulness and he was rewarded for the effort he made and the faith that he had.

The next story takes place one chapter later in Matthew 9:20-22. Jesus is on his way with his disciples to bring the daughter of a ruler back to life. Scripture tells us:

"Just then a woman who had been subject to bleeding for twelve years came up behind him and touched the edge of his cloak. She said to herself, 'If I only touch his cloak, I will be healed.' Jesus turned and saw her, 'Take heart, daughter' he said, 'your faith has healed you.' And the woman was healed from that moment."

This woman was condemned by Jewish religious law to believe that she was soiled and unworthy. Not only was she unclean, but anything she touched would have also been considered unclean. This meant it was her responsibility not to contaminate others. After twelve years, this woman decided that she could not, and would not remain hidden. She came to Jesus trembling; and falling down before Him, declared to herself in the presence of everyone watching why she had touched him, and He immediately healed her. But she had to get past the shame society made her feel and devote the effort to see and touch Him. She had to walk with intentional faithfulness.

The final story I want to share with you takes place in the Book of John 5:6-9. Jesus was on his way to Jerusalem for a feast of the Jews when he encountered a man who had been an invalid for thirty-eight years:

"When Jesus saw him lying there and learned that he had been in this condition for a long time, he asked him, 'Do you want to get well?' 'Sir,' the invalid replied, 'I have no one to help me into the pool when the water is stirred. While I am trying to get in, someone else goes down ahead of me.' Then Jesus said to him, 'Get up! Pick up your mat and walk.' At once the man was cured; he picked up his mat and walked.

In this story the man first had to have the faith that Jesus could heal him, and then he had to make the effort to get up, take his mat and walk into the life and destiny that Jesus had for him. He had to practice intentional faithfulness. And so, the question I have for you is, "Do you want to get well?" If so, you have to do your part. And because He loves you, you can trust that God will do His.

While it is imperative to offer our prayers up to God; simply wishing or hoping for things to change or come true won't make the changes happen. Dreaming also doesn't bring about needed change or improvements in our life. We have to make the transition from wanting to doing. We have to be intentional in our healing and walk into the plan that God has and truly desires for our lives. When you do that, you will regain the power and sense of self-worth that your abuser took away from you and that you lost from all of the abuse you endured. Being intentional in our healing isn't always the easiest path to take, but it will definitely provide the greatest results in the long run.

Focus on What Is Right with You

One of the things that can often hold us back from fully healing is that we spend too much time and effort looking into why or how we became a victim and what might be wrong within ourselves that could have possibly "caused" us to be abused. But this places our focus on ourselves as the problem instead of our abuser, which is where it truly and most deservedly should be.

The simple, plain truth is that you were abused because your abuser willfully chose to target you because of the good qualities you have, not because of anything that is wrong with you. All of your good qualities and personality traits such as being committed, encouraging, faithful, generous, loving, loyal, dependable, honest, and especially trustworthy is what your abuser chose to take advantage of. That's what attracted them to you in the first place.

And it's exactly those beautiful and amazing qualities that are going to help you recover from the abuse you received. You can use the same strength, commitment, determination and never-give-up attitude that enabled you to put up with your abuser's toxic behavior for so long, to help you overcome the trauma you endured and move on from this horrible episode in your life.

It's important to remember that it is fairly easy to lose your sense of self-dependability while you are experiencing the abuse, but your real self is still there and can be found again. You may not feel the complete return of the inner strength you have deep inside of you yet, but you can most assuredly draw from it when you need it again. In fact, you already drew from it to be able to leave your abuser in the first place!

17

Signs of Recovery and Healing

Recovery and healing from emotional abuse looks different for everyone. It may take several weeks or even months of no-contact after you have left your abuser before you even remotely start to feel relief. Your ability to avoid or limit contact and hold boundaries with your abuser going forward will also impact your ability to move on with your life.

Often your initial sense of relief after leaving is followed by a confusion of feelings toward your abuser and about leaving the relationship. However, you will know you are healing when you start to feel safer and more at ease with every aspect of your life. Here are some signs that you may be healing from emotional abuse:

You genuinely smile more and you find pleasure in the simplest of things. From the music you listen to, the food you eat, a book you read, time with friends or attending an event, you just seem to notice and be aware of good things more and more.

- You feel a sense of relief. Like a great weight has been taken off of your shoulders.
- You're getting better at identifying your feelings, controlling your emotions and dealing with them in a constructive manner.

- You are better able to concentrate on things, you find that you are more present in your conversations, and your mind tends to wander less.
- When things go wrong, you don't automatically blame yourself anymore. You are consciously able to acknowledge the role of others, yourself and outside factors in assessing problems and solutions.
- You do not spend your waking hours obsessing and worrying about your former partner. You don't follow them on social media and you have them blocked.
- You don't automatically second-guess yourself or ruminate about things. You are slowly getting your confidence back and you no longer wonder if you'll ever do anything right again.
- You are incorporating healthy habits into your lifestyle again that you may have forgotten about or put on hold. Exercise, healthy cooking, prayer, etc.
- You are starting to speak up without worrying what someone might say. You are finding your voice and speaking up about your opinion and needs.
- You're much less sensitive to rejection or slights. You are more aware of your triggers and you don't read emotions into things.
- You are able to set healthy boundaries with people and you no longer see other people's boundaries as a sign of rejection. You are able to connect with people in healthier and more respectful ways.
- You can acknowledge and take pride in what you do and handle well. You can once again celebrate your blessings, victories and progress.
- You can cope with things when you mess up, as well as deal with your missteps, mistakes and failures. You can show yourself compassion when you screw up and you no longer beat yourself up mentally and emotionally when you do.
- You feel more connected to your inner self, and less like you need to escape or distract yourself from problems. You are at peace with yourself.

- You are no longer ashamed of who you are, the relationship you allowed yourself to get in, the amount of time you stayed in it, or the abuse you endured.
- You no longer care about what your abuser is doing and you've come to understand that they probably will continue to repeat the same cycle of abuse with each person that comes into their life.
- Chronic physical symptoms (trauma) like headaches, stomach aches, indigestion and joint pain have begun to decrease in frequency and severity.
- You no longer care about how your abuser will react to your decisions. You don't worry whether your life choices will make them angry or make life inconvenient for them.
- You are now setting personal goals and beginning to achieve them. You have a plan for your future and you are taking positive steps to turn those plans into reality.
- You appreciate that self-care is something you need to participate in consistently. You realize it's ok to say no to people, take naps when you are exhausted and reduce some of your social engagements when you are feeling worn out.
- You no longer focus on problems, but on solutions. You realize that you have the power to change your circumstances, rather than remain defenseless against whatever stunts your abuser might be playing.
- You no longer obsess about what your abuser might think about you or what you are doing, and you no longer look to them for approval or appreciation.
- You see God in different things and places and you feel His presence in your life more. You are aware of His love for you and you take comfort in knowing that you are a child of God.
- You accept that there are people whose behavior is disturbingly toxic, you now know how to respond to it, and you no longer open yourself up to it.
- You realize just how strong you are. You were strong enough

to get out of the relationship, to get help to work through your feelings and pain, and set boundaries to keep your abuser as far away from you as possible.

- You've arrived as a survivor because you no longer tolerate anything or anyone that discounts your value. You have become your own best friend and advocate.

These are just some of the signs you can look to in order to assess your healing progress. There will be times that you make great strides moving forward and there will be other times that you take a few steps back. This is completely normal, so don't be too harsh on yourself. Healing from emotional abuse involves unlearning old habits, behaviors, responses and ways of thinking, and relearning healthy ones. There is no order to progress and this list doesn't represent one.

To fully heal from emotional recovery, you need to be committed to working on it for the long run. It takes time. Think of it as a marathon, not a sprint. Every survivor just wants to feel better again and move on, but it doesn't normally work that way. It's closer to taking baby steps because there is so much pain and emotion involved. Over time your old response to abuse default patterns will fall by the wayside and a new, smarter, happier, improved you will rise up. Have compassion on yourself and cheer yourself on as you notice the small and incremental changes. And most importantly, don't forget to celebrate along the way!

18

Moving Forward

Our initial awakening to the abuse we experienced and our subsequent healing from it is often a very gradual process as we start to understand, learn, and see clearly what has happened to us. It is a long road between our initial desire and hope for life-long relationship bliss, to the realization that what we are experiencing hurts and isn't healthy; and then the painful decision to leave the person we fell in love with and start the recovery process to heal from the terrible wounds our abuser has caused. But along the way you can rest assured that God will help you to confidently see what is real, fully understand what was said, remember what really happened and know without a doubt that what you experienced is true and deeply wrong.

Your experience was valid, no matter how hard people try to take that away from you. You deserve to be heard and to heal. You are not who your abuser said you are. You are who God says you are. I John 3:1 says,

> "See what kind of love the Father has given to us; that we should be called children of God; and so we are."

You are valuable and cherished because you are created by God, and

He will help you rebuild your life and your identity by helping you to fully accept who you truly are in Christ. It may take some time, but it will happen. Your life is now your own to live again, and you can take as much time as you want, on what you want, with whom you want, and where, when, and how you want to do it. You now have an opportunity to care for yourself on your own terms and there is no time limit for healing.

You will discover how to show yourself love in new and different ways. Despite all the lies your abuser told you, you will re-learn that self-love is not selfish but actually essential to you becoming a healthy and whole person again. You absolutely will feel better about yourself over time. Show yourself love by doing the things you want to do. Allow yourself a healthy indulgence every once in a while. You deserve it. Over time your heart and mind will reconcile and you will have your self-esteem back. Your new identity will slowly start to take shape and you can feel good about who you are again.

Love yourself by setting healthy boundaries with the people in your life, especially new people and new relationships. Boundaries are an essential part of practicing love with yourself. They allow you to define where your limits begin and end with the people around you. It is ok to disappoint someone and not feel guilty if they try to make you feel like you let them down. Your needs matter and it is your responsibility to decide who you choose to surround yourself with and with whom to have a relationship. You have every right to stand up for yourself and hold out for what you really want in life.

Possibly one of the hardest things to do in the recovery process is to try and make sense of the abuse you experienced, if it is even possible. At some point you will probably realize it's pretty much pointless to try. Because your abuser isn't a normal functioning human being, they don't think the same way most people would. After months of trying to understand her, I found that my abuser's motivation came down to a simple desire to exert and maintain power and control over me to attain the things she wanted out of our relationship. Once I came to peace with that simple fact, any deeper motivations or root causes she might have had ceased to matter anymore.

You probably will experience side effects from the trauma that was inflicted on you. You will have your good days and your bad days. This is completely normal. On the bad days, just let it all out and embrace every emotion you feel. It's a process and it is going to happen. Over time, you will have less of those days and eventually they will only become moments.

After all the time you were forced to only see the world through your abuser's perspective, you may experience a little confusion about how to start over again. That's when it's important to have trusted friends and family members to turn to. I would also strongly recommend finding a professional counselor/therapist you feel comfortable with to help you stabilize, process your emotions and move forward in your new life. When you get to the point that you can talk about what happened to you without getting really emotional, that's when you'll know that you are really starting to heal.

Just realize that the healing process can vary from person to person and can take many months and sometimes years. Everyone heals in their own time and there's really nothing you can do to rush it or force it. There may be times when you're not sure of yourself or the direction you are going. This is completely normal too. You went through months or years with your abuser being the only person in the relationship who was right, and whose opinion and authority was the only one that mattered. It may take time to regain your own perspective and feel comfortable about the decisions you make.

Remember that your abuser either tried to, or successfully changed your personal reality by altering how you saw yourself. They may have told you that you weren't capable, attractive or talented enough. That you were damaged goods, fortunate to have them since nobody else could possibly love you. They may have told you that you were forgetful, stupid, confused, crazy or any of the things that they themselves actually are. Abusive false narratives can sound like a lot of different things and they can be very damaging because they came from someone you loved and placed your trust in. That's always a tough thing to process.

These lies that were told to you and about you can often continue to affect the way you see yourself even after you've left your abuser. But once they're out of your life, it's time to take back your story. It's time to remember who you were before the relationship, where you came from and who you represent. It's time to remind yourself that you were a pretty special and amazing person before you met your abuser, and you still are that same person now. You just need to rediscover yourself.

And when you start to undo all of your abuser's lies and manipulations, it can feel like a spiritual awakening, especially when you have Jesus in the center of your life. He's always with us, and we'll always have His loving stamp of approval. You never have to try harder for Him to love you more, like you had to with your abuser. You never have to beg Him to stay. He never forces you to do anything, and you never have to feel compelled to do things you don't want to do. His unshakable love is who He is, and we can feel secure in Him. There's a passage in Hebrews 6:17-19 that I think completely sums up the difference between Jesus and your former abuser:

> "Because God wanted to make the unchanging nature of his purpose very clear to the heirs of what was promised, he confirmed it with an oath. God did this so that, by two unchangeable things in which it is impossible for God to lie, **we who have fled** to take hold of the hope set before us may be greatly encouraged. We have this hope as an anchor for the soul, firm and secure."

I want you to understand that you are worthy of God's love even if you don't feel like it. You are absolutely special to God. You are the apple of His eye. This means that you are at the very center of his thoughts, focus and protection. He loves you even when you are stubborn or caught in the worst of situations. His love and compassion for you remain constant and here is what He thinks about you:

- You are chosen. (Jeremiah 1:5, Ephesians 1:3-4)
- You are treasured. (Deuteronomy 14:2)
- You are irreplaceable. (1 Thessalonians 1:4)
- You are loved beyond compare. (1 John 4:10, 4:19)
- You are worth dying for. (1 John 3:16, Romans 5:7-9)
- You are His child. (1 John 3:1)
- You are secured for all eternity. (2 Corinthians 1:22, John 10:28-29)
- You are set free. (Romans 6:18, Galatians 5:1)
- You are precious to Him. (Isaiah 43:4)
- You are set apart. (John 15:19, 1 Peter 2:9)
- You are forgiven. (Ephesians 1:7, Romans 8:1)
- You cannot be separated from His Love. (Romans 8:35-39)

I want to encourage you to take some time to reflect on these truths about who you are. This is your identity in Christ. Just think about that for a minute. Let it sink in. Read this list and the Bible references often, and remind yourself of your true identity. All you have to do is ask for it if you haven't already done so (see page).

Jesus is the all-time healer of broken hearts. He healed the broken heart of the woman at the well who was on her sixth relationship in John 4:1-26. He forgave and restored a woman who was caught in the act of adultery in John 8:3-11. In the Book of Joel 2:25-27 He says He can supernaturally restore the years the locusts (our abusers) have eaten away" and take away the shame you may feel from being in an abusive relationship. In Isaiah 61:3 God tells us:

"He will replace our ashes of grief with a crown of beauty."

You are amazing and precious in God's eyes, and you can hold your head up high because you now have a crown of beauty on it.

There's one other thing I want you to grab hold of and that is: no matter how stuck or confused you might still feel right now, there is a great future out there waiting for you and it will be better than anything you experienced before. That's because God has great plans for you. Jeremiah 29:11 says:

"For I know the plans I have for you, declares the Lord, plans to prosper you and not to harm you, plans to give you hope and a future."

That is a promise you can count on. This is a gift that your Father in heaven has given specifically for you. Claim it and embrace it.

Rebuilding your identity and your personal story is a process that takes time. Regardless of where you take your story from this point, all the choices are yours now. You are no longer a victim. You are a survivor and you should stand tall and be proud. It no longer matters how your abuser got into your life, why you stayed in the relationship, why you tolerated their abuse or how long you stayed. What matters is you got out. You made it. And you're free.

Finding a Good Counselor/Therapist

A successful treatment program starts with finding a counselor/therapist you can trust and with whom you can feel comfortable. Ask friends for recommendations and take the time to look up counselor bios on their websites to get a feel for one you might like. Most counselors are more than willing to allow you a quick interview over the phone so you can get a feel for them. A good counselor should work together with you in a collaborative fashion to develop an understanding of the problems and challenges you face, and to develop a treatment strategy. Most reputable therapists incorporate a number of different therapies to help you with your recovery. And if for some reason you don't hit it off after your first few sessions, find another one.

Cognitive Behavioral Therapy

(CBT) is a form of treatment that is effective for a range of problems including depression, anxiety disorders, alcohol and drug use problems, marital problems, eating disorders, and severe mental illness. It is based on several core principles with the belief that psychological problems are based, in part, on faulty or unhelpful ways of thinking and on learned patterns of unhelpful behavior. CBT treatment usually involves efforts to change thinking patterns. People suffering from psychological problems can learn better ways of coping with them, thereby relieving their symptoms and becoming more effective in their lives. It helps clients gain a better understanding of their behavior, gain a greater sense of confidence, helps them face their fears instead of avoiding them and gives them problem-solving skills to cope with difficult situations.

CBT places an emphasis on helping individuals learn to be their own therapists. Through exercises in each counseling session as well as "homework" exercises outside of the sessions, clients are helped to develop coping skills, whereby they can learn to change their own thinking, problematic emotions, and behavior. It helps the client move forward by developing more effective ways of coping with life.

Person-Centered Therapy

(PCT) diverges from the traditional model of the therapist as the expert, and instead focuses toward an empathetic approach that empowers and motivates the client in the therapeutic process. The therapy is based on the belief that every human being strives for and has the capacity to fulfill his or her own potential. Rather than viewing people as inherently flawed, with problematic behaviors and thoughts that require treatment, person-centered therapy identifies that each person has the capacity and desire for personal growth and change. At the heart of this therapeutic approach is the concept of self-actualization - where a counselor helps the client gain self-understanding for altering their basic attitudes, and self-directed behavior.

The person-centered therapist learns to recognize and trust the potential in each client, providing them with empathy and unconditional positive regard to help facilitate change. The therapist avoids directing the course of therapy by following the client's lead whenever possible. Instead, the therapist offers support, guidance, and structure so that the client can discover personalized solutions within themselves.

Internal Family Systems Therapy

(IFS) is an approach to psychotherapy that identifies and addresses multiple sub-personalities or families within each person's mental system. These sub-personalities consist of wounded parts and painful emotions such as anger and shame, and parts that try to control and protect the person from the pain of the wounded parts. The sub-personalities are often in conflict with each other and with one's core Self, a concept that describes the confident, compassionate, whole person that is at the core of every individual. IFS focuses on healing the wounded parts and restoring mental balance and harmony by changing the dynamics that create discord among the sub-personalities and the Self.

IFS therapy is used to treat individuals, couples, and families. It is an evidence-based approach that has been shown to be effective for treating a variety of conditions and their symptoms, such as depression, anxiety, phobias, panic, and physical health conditions such as rheumatoid arthritis, as well as improving general functioning and well-being.

Recommended Reading

When Sorry Isn't Enough
by Gary Chapman & Jennifer Thomas
Making things right with those you love.

Safe People
by Dr. Henry Cloud & Dr. John Townsend
How to find relationships that are good for you, and avoid those that aren't.

Whole Again
by Jackson MacKenzie
Healing your heart and rediscovering your true self after toxic relationships and emotional abuse.

Why Won't You Apologize?
By Harriet Lerner, PH.D.
Healing big betrayals and everyday hurts.

The Power of Forgiveness
by Emily J. Hooks
A guide to healing and wholeness.

Transitions – Making Sense of Life's Changes
by William Bridges
Strategies for coping with the difficult, painful and confusing times in your life.

Restored – Experience Life With Jesus
by Neil T Anderson
Experience the life you were meant to live, restored in Christ.

Love & Respect
By Dr. Emerson Eggerichs
The Love she most desires, The Respect he desperately needs.

Acknowledgments

I have been blessed throughout my personal healing process by a number of friends and family without whose constant support and encouragement, my recovery would have probably taken much longer. A very special thank you goes out to my daughter Alena; my friends Len, Jan, Mike, Kerry, Mark, Adam, Matt, Jared, Jennifer, Valerie, Debbie, Margie and my counselor Darren.

I would like to thank the following artists whose music I found especially comforting and healing during my recovery period: Joe Bonamassa, Haevn, Switchfoot, JP Cooper, David Gilmour, Shallou, Seal, John Mayer, Santana, Chris Rea, Ritchie Kotzen, Glenn Hughes, Scorpions, and Michael W Smith.

Finally, to God, who makes all good things happen and without whose grace this book would have never been possible. Thank You Jesus, for Your never-ending love and for healing me.

Greyson James

For more helpful resources on surviving and healing from emotional abuse and toxic relationships, please visit my website at:

FreedomFromAbuse.com

Also by
GREYSON JAMES

Surviving a Toxic and Abusive Relationship

It is estimated that one out of every seven people in the world suffer from one or more of the Cluster B personality disorders. No matter if they suffer from antisocial, borderline, histrionic or narcissistic personality disorder; all emotional abusers have this in common: unhealthy, superficial, inappropriate or completely nonexistent human emotions and extremely abusive, erratic, dysfunctional and toxic behavior.

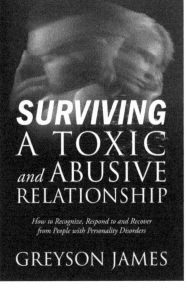

Emotional abusers use anger, aggression, deceit, exaggeration, seduction, manipulation and excessive emotion to get what they want and to hide who they really are. Most are so good at what they do, and so relentless at pursuing and achieving what they desire, that most of the time their victims won't truly realize what is happening to them until they become so isolated, hurt, confused, and disoriented, that they lose all sense of reality and self-identity.

Emotional abuse can happen to anyone, but it is a personal hell through which no one should ever have to suffer. Honest, open, insightful and thoughtfully written from the first-hand experience and perspective of an abuse survivor, this book will not only help you identify behaviors that can lead to emotional abuse, but it will also give you the ability to recognize, avoid, escape and recover from its various forms, in all of its subtlety and expressions. It also provides an understanding of why people with Cluster B disorders do what they do, simultaneously shedding light on these disorders that are so often behind mental and emotional abuse.

Learn more at:
www.outskirtspress.com/survivingatoxicandabusiverelationship